LET'S
MOVE
ON

BEYOND FEAR &
FALSE PROPHETS

VICENTE FOX

WITH SULAY HERNÁNDEZ-ELHUSSEIN

A SAVIO REPUBLIC BOOK
An Imprint of Post Hill Press

Let's Move On:
Beyond Fear & False Prophets
© 2018 by Vicente Fox
All Rights Reserved

ISBN: 978-1-68261-543-0
ISBN (eBook): 978-1-68261-5-447

Interior Design and Composition by Greg Johnson/Textbook Perfect

posthillpress.com
New York • Nashville
Published in the United States of America

To America: Resist!
The dream of freedom will not fade into the night.
Hope always wins, love always prevails.

Contents

What Happened?

"He who puts out his hand to stop the wheel of history will have his fingers crushed."

—LECH WAŁĘSA, former president of Poland

A S OF THIS MOMENT, it is unclear what really happened with the 2016 United States presidential election. There were two candidates. One was former senator and secretary of state Hillary Clinton, a woman who had dedicated more than forty years of her life to the application of law and public service. She was, by every single measure, the most qualified candidate for the office of the presidency who has ever existed—man or woman, of any political party. The other candidate was Donald Trump, a notoriously flashy New York businessman, heir to his father's wealth, with a reputation for ethically and morally ambiguous dealings. Trump had absolutely no government experience of any kind. He'd had multiple marriages, filed six bankruptcies, and been involved in over 3,500 legal actions both in state and federal courts.

The choice for the American people was clear. At least it was clear to me and to everyone else around the globe who waited for the new leader of the free world. It had been a long year and a half of one of the most divisive modern U.S. presidential campaigns many of us had ever witnessed. The reason for its ugliness was Donald Trump. The man seemed to take the air out of every room he walked into. His campaign was a freak show, complete with insults hurled at political opponents, calls for violence against protestors, a preoccupation with his hand size and crowd size (Donald, you have tiny hands. Sorry. Remember, it's not the size that counts), and a maniacal focus on what he called the "dishonest" mainstream media. Journalists were placed in press pens at the back of his rallies and subjected to taunts and threats from Trump supporters frenzied by his screams about "fake news." Trump joked about killing reporters, said Clinton was corrupted by her years in Washington, suggested she be "taken care of by the Second Amendment people," and offered to pay the legal fees of supporters who punched protestors. His speeches had no substance; they were delivered in incomplete sentences devoid of any real plans, just promises that complex problems would be fixed easily and quickly, punctuated by chants of "USA!" and "Lock her up!" His supporters applauded his brash, unrefined delivery. Pundits began calling him a "blue-collar billionaire." His ignorance was praised as evidence that he truly was a "Washington outsider" who would drain the D.C. swamp of corruption. His supporters claimed that even without any history of public service and despite having inherited millions of dollars and being mired in seemingly countless financial scams, he was truly "a man of the people." I wasn't as concerned with

Trump's style (I've been told a time or two I can be a hothead myself) as I was horrified by his actual message.

This man was serious trouble—the kind of trouble I knew a lot about. I was president of Mexico from 2000 to 2006, elected in what was considered the first truly democratic election since 1929. For most of the twentieth century, Mexico was a conservative country run by the nationalist and xenophobic PRI political party. The PRI controlled our lives—everything from the media to what we could learn, buy, and eat. They controlled the people's dreams, because they alone decided what was possible. They kept the Mexican people in their place with propaganda about "the evil American empire" and the country's being taken over by pizza, hamburgers, rock 'n' roll, Motown, and Budweiser. The PRI wrapped up their authoritarian government in patriotism so anyone who disagreed was anti-Mexican. And they silenced dissenters by any means necessary—including making people disappear and rigging elections. I know an authoritarian regime when I see one because I lived it. And I knew Trump was selling bullshit wrapped in the American flag.

Donald Trump announced his candidacy for president of the United States on June 16, 2015, at Trump Tower with a speech that was nothing but a brazen repudiation of modern American ideals and values. The buffoon rode down an escalator to an adoring crowd filled with paid extras and began a verbal tirade of falsehoods and insults against practically the entire world. First, his political opponents were elsewhere "sweating like dogs" because they didn't have air conditioners like he did, the country was in "serious trouble," China was "killing" the U.S., Mexico was "not our friend" and sending people with "lots of problems" who were "bringing drugs," and "bringing crime," who were "rapists" (and some, he assumed, were "good people"). He disparaged both South and Central America, and stated that "Islamic terrorism [was] eating up large portions of the Middle East. They've become rich. I'm in competition with them." Trump complained that terrorists had bought a hotel in Syria "without paying interest" and the United States was stupid for not taking the Iraqis' oil.

The message was that America was "dying," America needed money, all the other countries were laughing at America, and Americans were "losers." China and Mexico were stealing American jobs. Not even America's nuclear arsenal worked properly. As a businessman, Trump was going to fix all of these problems and fund his campaign with his very own money. He would renegotiate old trade deals and make new deals for America, get rid of the fraud and the waste in government. He promised to build a great wall on the Southern border and have Mexico pay for it. He ended the speech by saying that the American Dream was dead and that he would "make America great again." In this speech, Trump took the wealthiest, truest democracy on earth and redefined it as an ailing country full of unemployed citizens, foreign criminals, terrorists, and overall losers. Empirical evidence to the contrary didn't matter, because it all came from "intellectual elites" and "fake news." Nothing was true except for what Trump said. His speech was so unhinged, many thought Trump's candidacy was a publicity stunt—maybe to get attention for his various real estate projects and potential television deals.

To me, Trump has always been the quintessential embodiment of the "ugly American" trope: a vulgar money-grubber who made his wealth off the backs of people he would never sit down with and kept his wealth by shamelessly manipulating the legal system. Trump represented everything that anti-American ideologues feared—unleashed capitalism, imperialism, a loss of morals and traditional family values. He wasn't qualified to lead a real business, much less a country. Trump clearly didn't understand how the world had evolved or how it worked; he didn't know much about anything past his golden-walled towers except how to take advantage of others. Trump was a joke. But I wasn't laughing, because I also knew just how much Trump's message could appeal to the part of human nature that was afraid of change. In a country like the United States, an aspirational society that told people they could reach the top if they worked hard enough, Trump's "You're losing because someone else is winning" was a seductive message. It provided an easy answer for those who had been left behind in the globalized economy. This particular brand of "us versus them," the message of fear and hate and envy and greed, was a disease that, once stoked, wouldn't heal easily or soon. His promises to "make America great again" with a return to the "good ol' days" were siren calls to the racist, isolationist, anti-immigration impulses that every country must struggle to rise from in order to truly be great.

To his toxic brew of nationalist politics, Donald Trump, an infamous womanizer, also added rampant misogyny. He was caught on camera admitting to grabbing women without their consent, and defended himself against multiple sexual assault accusations by saying the victims were not attractive enough for him to touch. During a live Republican debate, he said that candidate Carly Fiorina had a face "no one would vote for" and Hillary Clinton lacked "presidential looks," "strength," and "stamina." In a truly bizarre publicity stunt, he brought the women who had allegedly been romantically involved with Hillary Clinton's husband to the final presidential debate. Trump knew he could never win a debate on ideas and principles; he had to make it personal and mean-spirited. Despite it all, Trump held onto the Republican nomination. He then seemed to crown himself king and supreme leader, stating that he alone could fix all of America's problems. His supporters did not need to believe what their eyes and ears told them about the world, but only what he said, because he was their "voice." In short, Trump's behavior, his utter lack of intellectual curiosity, gravitas, and personal restraint, had stripped the decency and respect from what was supposed to be a dignified public discourse between would-be leaders of the most developed country on earth.

Why do I care so much about the United States and Donald Trump? Well, what would you do if your neighbor's house were on fire? Would you sit there and watch just because it's not your house? Or would you try to help? I feel morally obligated to help, not just because helping others in need is the right thing to do, but because if you don't do something, your house will soon catch fire too. Mexico and the United States have a long and complicated history, but we are friends and allies. We have made great progress in the past two decades, and I'm not going to sit by and let Trump insult Mexico and its people and all of the work the two countries have done together. In an interview in February 2016 with journalist Jorge Ramos, whom Trump threw out of a live campaign event the previous year and told to "go back to Univision," I sent Trump a message in his own style:

"*Mexico is not paying for your fucking wall.*" I also said he was an ignorant egomaniac and a false prophet, and if he was so rich, he should pay for the wall himself. Trump demanded an apology, which I gave because I believe in forgiveness and compassion, but I asked that Trump reconsider his stance on Mexico and apologize for his blatant disrespect of the Mexican people. He never did apologize in return, because Trump lacks the moral compass that would make him a true leader. Regardless, I knew a bully when I saw one, and knew how to deal with bullies— head on. I started #NoFuckingWall trending on Twitter and promised to be Donald Trump's shadow. I had a voice and I had privilege, and I was going to confront this monster at every turn until the election, where I was sure the will of the American people would send Trump and his goons back to their corrupt backroom real estate deals and barrage of lawsuits, and leave the governing to those who cared. I knew the United States was better than Donald Trump. There was no way Trump would be elected president.

Tragically, on November 9, 2016, the impossible happened. Donald Trump won more of the electoral college than Hillary Clinton, while she won the popular vote by almost three million, the widest margin by a losing candidate in the history of the United States. Many say that American-style democracy is the most representative of the will of the people, but I think that it is a stain upon the country that the candidate who won the majority of the people's vote lost the election. The 2016 election will forever be tainted, and nothing will get that stain out except a serious review of the electoral system. Trump, of course, claimed he lost the popular vote only because three to five million "illegals" voted for Hillary—an utterly absurd claim in a country where half of the citizens do not go to the polls. Those who do want to vote often encounter draconian voter ID laws that prevent them from doing so, and gerrymandered districts are designed to give certain parties political advantages. I agree with former president Barack Obama and many others— America doesn't have a voter fraud problem; it has a voter problem.

What we do know today is that America might also have a Putin-fraud problem. Seventeen U.S. intelligence agencies have confirmed that a Kremlin-led network of computer hackers managed to steal campaign data and generally disrupt the elections through a carefully planned disinformation campaign. How many votes were affected by the constant barrage of conspiracy theories, fake propaganda, and leaked Clinton campaign emails is hard to quantify, but Trump's populist appeal to ill-informed voters, many of whom harbored racist, anti-immigrant, and misogynist views, combined with questions about Clinton's handling of classified emails and the outdated electoral college system proved too much to overcome. Trump and his campaign associates are now under FBI investigation as to whether they directly colluded with the Kremlin to sway the election in his favor, but only time will tell the truth on this.

Despite the suspicions, the fact remained that Trump was elected and Mexico would have to dance with the ugly American. Setting aside the issue of Russian interference, I called Trump an illegitimate president because of his constant lies, his lack of knowledge, and his anti-American rhetoric. I carried a heavy heart for those immigrants from all over the world who were now gripped by terror at Trump's presidency, and for all of our allies who now feared destabilization or even another world war. I wrote an op-ed the day after the election, in which I stated, "We, the citizens of the World, face one challenge today; to keep working to prevent, at all costs, Donald Trump causing more harm to the United States and the rest of the world."

The United States is not perfect, but it brings so much hope to people around the world yearning for the freedom so many take for granted. Trump is a menace to democracy, a menace to the very ideals of compassionate leadership that have come to define America. Make no mistake, the United States is the strongest nation on earth, and the entire world depends on its leadership, but things like "freedom," "liberty," and "justice" are only as true and as strong as those who believe and work to keep these ideals alive. Millions of Americans have woken up from their stupor and are standing up for their rights against this wannabe tyrant. Each and every one of them is part of The Resistance.

The Women's March, held on January 21, 2017, one day after the presidential inauguration, became the largest ever single-day protest in history. There were sister marches all over the world, including in Mexico. Millions of women, their partners, and their children took to the streets to protest Donald Trump's terrifying agenda to rip families apart through deportations, destroy environmental protections, and strip the most vulnerable of basic civil rights. Protestors have shown up at every airport in the country, demanding that immigrants be allowed in. Each and every one of these protestors is committed to the fight. In a somewhat controversial statement, the Dalai

Lama once said, "Western women will save the world." I've met the Dalai Lama, and I think he's onto something. Hillary Clinton should have been the president of the United States, but I know it makes her proud that women lead the The Resistance. I am proud to support and stand with them against the forces of hate and bigotry that Trump has unleashed.

I decided to write these pages because the safety and success both of Mexico and the United States are inextricably tied. I can see our neighbor's house is smoking and will soon be on fire; it is my moral obligation and duty to speak out. We have come too far together to throw it all away on one man's delusions of grandeur and willful ignorance. The following are my meditations on the current state of the world, the challenges we face, and the ways to overcome them. I have seen much in my seventy-five years on this earth, both as a public and private person—as a boy who grew up on a ranch, and as a salesman turned political activist who eventually became leader of a country. As president, I traveled the world to promote Mexico's democracy and Mexico's interests—from the White House to the Kremlin, from the Vatican to Castro's dining room, from Tony Blair's fireside to Nelson Mandela's offices. I have gone from presidential palaces to slums, spoken with Chinese farmers, Arab leftists, African dignitaries, those who are rich and those who are extremely poor. I am writing straight from my heart to yours. Through all my successes and failures, there is one thing I know is true—if humanity is to survive, it will not be because we built walls, but only because we built bridges.

PART 1

WHERE WE ARE TODAY

Globalization, Immigration, and Walls

CHAPTER 1

Globalization and Trade

"Geography has made us neighbors. History has made us friends. Economics has made us partners, and necessity has made us allies. Those whom God has so joined together, let no man put asunder."

–JOHN F. KENNEDY, addressing the Canadian Parliament

A FAMOUS AMERICAN BUSINESSMAN ONCE said, "I know that doesn't make it any easier for people whose jobs have been outsourced overseas, but if a company's only means of survival is by farming jobs outside its walls, then sometimes it's a necessary step. The other option might be to close its doors for good." That famous American businessman was Donald Trump.

This is the same man who burst onto the political stage shrieking about China's "raping the U.S.," painting Mexico as a job-stealing enemy, and decrying the World Trade Organization as unfair to the United States. He promised to label China a currency manipulator and bring legal action against it; he promised to rip up the North American Free Trade Agreement between Mexico,

Canada, and the U.S. and renegotiate bilateral trade deals with every country. In his speech accepting the Republican nomination for president, Trump said, "Americanism, not globalism, will be our credo." Soon after being elected, Trump pulled out from further discussions of President Obama's signature trade proposal, the Trans Pacific Partnership Agreement, which, arguably, would have cemented the United States' leadership position in the developing world economy. Trump's mantras were "America first" and "Hire American, buy American." The United States would make and buy its own stuff, and he was going to bring back all the jobs that had gone overseas because of the evil globalists. Trump was here to save America just by the sheer power of his will and business savvy, because only he understood the system and only he knew how to negotiate things fairly.

It is a fact that Donald Trump has negotiated his way into six bankruptcies over the years. We also know that the majority of Trump-branded products are made in at least twelve other countries and that his worldwide residential towers, hotels, wineries, and private-club golf courses employ both legal and undocumented immigrants from all over the world. "We will no longer surrender this country and its people to the false song of globalism," he thundered, but Trump's business is literally selling his name to anyone who will pay. The irony is not just that he is a direct beneficiary of the globalization economy that he puts down as unfair to the American people but also that way before he came along, America had become the richest country on earth by selling the idea of globalization to the rest of the world.

International trade has been around for centuries, but for our purposes we'll use the period after World War II as the beginning of what we understand as modern globalization. Soon after the global tragedy that was World War II, America convinced the entire world that the only way to have real sociopolitical stability and economic development was through open markets. One had only to see the horrors that lay inside Germany's walls under Hitler's Nazi regime to see the results of unhinged nationalist and protectionist policies. The European Union was created to heal the divisions that had devastated the continent and led to millions of lost lives. The thrust of the idea was that countries that were economically, socially, and politically interdependent would be less likely to enter into conflict. The United States also contributed to the EU with a financial aid package known as the Marshall Plan. The goal was to help repair the war-torn continent and, of course, ease trading regulations and stop the spread of communism. The binding together of countries based on shared needs is, in a general sense, the definition of globalization.

It is no secret that I fully support global economic exchange. I fell in love with the American business model in my early adulthood and greatly admired corporate titans like Henry Ford and Andrew Carnegie—the men who made the cars and engines that helped the world turn. As soon as I left college in 1964, I started working at the Ford Motor Company, but office work did not suit this farm boy. I needed open air and to be close to the land. I had attended Mexico's Ibero-American University, a pillar of Jesuit education, and was one of the heirs to a thousand-acre Spanish-style hacienda, but I accepted an offer to work for Coca-Cola driving a delivery truck and selling Coke door to door. I drove all over the entire country of Mexico, competing with the Pepsi drivers, interacting with the incredibly diverse people of my country. The PRI government, of course, feared that the "*gringo* drink" would displace the traditional Mexican sugared drinks, but it never did. It just created another drink for Mexicans to love. Because of my travels, I was able to touch the hearts and minds of people from all walks of life, and this would later serve me well when I went into politics. I spent fifteen years with Coca-Cola and rose through the ranks to become the president of its Mexican division. At the upper echelons of the corporate ladder, my business travels took me all over the world, and I could see with my own eyes how much the free-market democracies prospered while Mexico was left behind, the majority of its people hungry and uneducated, walled off, and fearful of an invasion by the outside world.

Early trade started between tribes of hunter-gatherers and small villages exchanging food and tools. These kinds of exchanges obviously allowed people to learn new skills and are responsible for the development of humankind. On a larger scale, nations used to be self-sustaining because they had to be; they didn't know any other way. They produced and consumed for themselves. As time went on, nations realized they couldn't produce everything they needed or wanted. But going from small domestic exchanges to trading on an international level had its problems—there were, of course, some dishonest practices in which people didn't quite get what they paid for. Trade regulations were put in place to minimize these issues and bring transparency to commerce—to ensure "fair trade." This set of laws and policies is what we know of today as the World Trade Organization.

Open trade paved the way for established corporations to invest in developing countries. These developing countries would use these investments ostensibly to create better living conditions and higher wages for their citizens, who were then in a better position to buy more things. Countries like Japan sold to the U.S., the U.S. to Brazil, and on to Africa—everyone selling and buying, everyone generating jobs and higher wages. The United States was able to sell everything from Coca-Cola, Pepsi, McDonald's, Ford, Chrysler, and so forth, and eventually to more information-based technology like computers and Google all around the world (and spread the message of "democracy" and "freedom" along the way).

Separate trade agreements between countries were born out of necessity and convenience. One of the largest trade agreements was the North American Free Trade Agreement (NAFTA), kicked off by President Ronald Reagan and finally signed into law by President Bill Clinton. The United States, Mexico, and Canada created a platform on which they could trade more easily and compete with the giant economies of the European Union and China. Tariffs were removed, which was an enormous benefit for consumers. If an avocado cost $1 in Mexico, it cost $1 in the United States and Canada. With a 20 percent trading tariff, American and Canadian consumers would have to pay $1.20. Because we shared a huge mass of land, our three countries could also produce products together more quickly and cheaply that could then be sold to others.

With NAFTA, two developed countries bound their economies with an emerging one for the first time, and Mexico flourished. We learned to use our human capital, created universities and other skill-learning centers, and threw ourselves wholeheartedly into the trade game. Standards of living got better with rising wages and a new sphere of workers who could now afford education for their children. And yes, sometimes things seemed to be working better for Mexico than they were for the U.S. The United States liked and could afford to buy our products, and took advantage of a young, cheap labor force, while Mexico, still a developing country, at times could not buy American products if the dollar was too strong. Trade and currency valuation go hand in hand and are complicated matters but, in general, developing countries develop faster than a country that's already developed—but that's because they have more room for growth. Anyone who understands business knows it is much easier to grow a start-up than it is to maintain consistent growth of a business that is already doing really well. This is why Mexico's GDP could grow at 5 to 8 percent per year while America's grew at 2 to 3 percent.

Donald Trump and politicians on both the right and left sides of the conversation are being disingenuous when they shill for votes with antiglobalist talking points among disillusioned constituents who have lost their jobs. The truth is that global trade actually makes it possible for exporting companies to pay higher wages overall to their employees, because outsourcing lower-skill sections of the manufacturing line also protects high-paying jobs for those who have specific expert-level skills or are in middle- or high-level management positions.

Consider that there are millions of jobs in the United States just waiting to be filled. The problem isn't a lack of jobs; the problem is the large gap between the skills certain workers have and the ones needed for the emerging jobs market. The bottom line is that whether it's a large corporation or a small home-based business, every business is in a relentless pursuit of growth. The other bottom line is that consumers relentlessly demand higher-quality, lower-priced products. There are many people, including both U.S. and Mexican citizens, who have lost their jobs, not to a foreign national but to computers and robots, which are simply more efficient. Should we destroy robots and computers and return to the "good ol' days"? That would be ridiculous—just as it would be ridiculous for hardworking American citizens to pay $10 for an avocado grown on U.S. soil when they can buy one for $2 grown on their southern neighbor's land and save $8 in their bank accounts.

It is true that in the short term, it is easy to define "winners" and "losers" in the globalized economy—the winners have jobs and the losers lose them. But nothing is that simple. Despite the United States' having the largest economy on earth, millions of U.S. citizens are still living in poverty or at least living one or two paychecks away from it. These are people who are not inheriting millions, people from all racial and ethnic backgrounds who work hard every single day, for whom the benefits of a first-class education that would place them on a higher rung on the economic ladder is not realistically within reach. Trump was supposedly catapulted into the presidency by a relatively small base of fed-up majority of working and middle-class white people suffering from a disease called "economic anxiety." Their anxiety was based on the fear that swarthy foreigners were coming to take their jobs and that good-paying jobs would keep going overseas to countries full of swarthy foreigners. This smoldering fire of "economic anxiety" is rooted in racist ideology, and income inequality is the gasoline poured on it. The fact is that in the richest country on earth, it is the rich who keep getting richer, while the poor can barely hang on.

I believe that it is every country's responsibility to prepare its citizenry for the future. Globalization can be a win-win for everyone—a rising tide lifts all boats, regardless of how big or small your particular boat is—but we all have to become better at laying a strong foundation on which the people can navigate these new waters. Economic reforms are painful for everyone in the beginning, especially so for developing countries, and even more painful for the poor, because they have limited resources to begin with. In Mexico, it was clear that those closest to the border, where the majority of new industry was located, benefitted most and faster from NAFTA than those living in central and southern Mexico.

In the early days of NAFTA, Mexican farmers were hit the hardest. Their small, traditional farms just couldn't compete with the scale of agriculture in the U.S., which produced much more quickly and effectively. It was the same with industries that were absolutely booming in the early '90s, such as manufacturing and energy. Mexico just didn't have a workforce that was educated enough to jump into the information age. But we've spent the past two decades educating ourselves, and the wealth has spread, but we have much work to do in decentralizing this progress. Consider that almost 15 percent of Mexico's population are Mayan, indigenous people who live primarily in the southern part of the country and are the poorest. They don't speak Spanish, which makes it incredibly difficult for them to integrate into the new economic system, similar to Mexican immigrants who must learn English in order to fully succeed in the United States.

So, we Mexicans understand how important the need to adapt is and how important it is for different social classes to feel they are both contributing to and benefitting from the riches of globalization. The rich folks don't seem to understand the lessons of history—when the poor, who are absolutely essential to the economy, don't feel the benefits of prosperity, there will always be unrest and some kind of revolution. We can soften the impact of immediate losses if the government provides workers with the educational tools and social safety nets that give them the ability to adapt and the freedom and security to innovate.

There is no doubt that globalization has made this world better—it has made it possible for us to share ideas, goods, and technologies that have helped bring millions out of poverty and taken more millions into the middle class. Hillary Clinton said, "There are four billion cell phones in use today, many in the hands of market vendors, rickshaw drivers, and others who've historically lacked access to education and opportunity. Information networks are a great leveler, and we should use them together to help lift people out of poverty and give them a freedom from want." She's right. We have more information available today than at any other point in human history. We have the tools, but we have to know how to use them. Access to the internet means nothing to someone who can't read or who can't afford a computer.

In the same vein, what good are millions of available jobs to a United States worker who doesn't have the skills to fill them, the resources to pay for a new education, or the means to move to a different city? Why doesn't Donald Trump budget federal money to fund new retraining programs and revitalize existing ones instead of wasting money on more military and useless wars and unnecessary tax cuts for the rich? It's hard for forty- or fifty-year-old people to be laid off a job they've done their entire lives, but they must be given a safety net so they can have the opportunity to reinvent themselves without the fear of losing their home and pension. Trump says he has billions of dollars. True leaders put their money where their mouth is. Why not invest a few of those billions into a fund that pays a good salary to laid-off workers while they attend retraining programs?

The bottom line is that jobs like coal mining are dying, and despite Trump's promises, they are not coming back. The coal mines are bad for the environment, and they are literally killing the people who work in them. Why not have programs in place that help displaced workers integrate into the booming emerging renewable-energy markets? Hillary Clinton told the truth when she said the coal industry was going to be put out of business. It's outdated and dangerous and the energy industry is evolving—marvelous innovations continue to emerge with solar energy, wind, and hydropower. Instead of speaking the truth, Donald Trump promised to bring back coal mines and perpetuated the myth that foreigners were at fault.

We know that if companies have to choose between paying $5 per hour in Mexico or paying $18 per hour in the U.S., they will choose whatever continues to grow their business, because the market and shareholders demand it. Car companies know that if they don't streamline their production costs, people will simply choose a cheaper brand that is of a similar quality. I don't know too many people who are willing to pay an extra $20,000 for a car simply because all of the parts were made in America. The market moves according to Adam Smith's invisible hand, and governmental regulations provide the guardrails. Governments don't create jobs or single-handedly change an economy. The market is dictated by private-sector investors and fueled by consumer demand.

Trump keeps harping on the large trade deficit between America and Mexico, currently at around $60 billion. Yet, the deficit with China is $350 billion, with the European Union around $100 billion, with Japan around $90 billion. Why is Donald Trump picking this huge fight with Mexico, a neighbor? Not only are Mexico's cities filled with thriving Fortune 500 franchises, but we are on the way to becoming the United States' second-biggest customer overall. Not only have we bought trillions of dollars' worth of products since the beginning of NAFTA, and millions of Americans are employed precisely because of our trading partnership, but we also work with the United States to help secure the border against terrorism and the flow of drugs.

As I said before, it makes sense to work with your neighbor, and there are moral and logical arguments that compel us to do so. Geopolitically speaking, the well-being of a nation is dependent on the safety and well-being of the countries that border it. It would be terrible if America shared a border with a destitute, conflicted country. This is the lesson at the heart of the European Union. Imagine the national security nightmare if America, the richest country on earth, had not only to protect itself from enemies overseas but also deal with a starving country right next door. It would make no sense.

President Bill Clinton, who helped usher in NAFTA, understood this. Both he and Hillary Clinton were great allies of Mexico and won the hearts of all Mexicans during our economic crisis in 1994. The same year that we entered into the historic NAFTA agreement, a series of political shock waves that included a violent uprising and the assassination of a presidential candidate along with some governmental missteps led to the severe devaluation of the peso. Overnight, Mexico lost half its value—homes, cars, savings, everything was lost. President Clinton had a decision to make. Let Mexico sink or help it swim. He decided to extend a hand. Mexico received a $50 billion bailout, which we committed to paying back within ten years. I'm proud to say Mexico paid it back in just a year and a half. That is the nature of our commitment and the value we place on our relationship with the United States. President Clinton's compassion and leadership during that time are a perfect example of how far the United States had come from its former image as a colonizer and "evil empire" to a cooperative nation whose democratic ideals solidified its position as leader of the free world.

It saddens me deeply to witness the rise of antiglobalist, antitrade sentiment spread across the world over the past decade by messianic leaders who appeal to the worst parts of human nature. How did America, with its expansionist history, modernity, wealth, and access to information turn its back on everything it told the world? We know that countries who have walled themselves off, selling dreams of "*We are first*" and "*We are only"* end in utter devastation. History provides us many examples, Venezuela being the most obvious and recent—a previously rich country that followed demagogue Hugo Chavez into the abyss. I'm not saying that Trump *is* America's Hugo Chavez; I'm saying Trump's rhetoric has the same tone as Chavez's, and his showmanship and misguided narrow populist views are dangerously similar. False prophets like these begin to slowly erode the culture of a nation, the shared beliefs and ideals, until the values of the country come tumbling down and descend into chaos.

There is poverty everywhere; there is certainly poverty in the United States, and there is poverty in Mexico—although Mexico's situation, as a whole, is much worse than the United States'. But both countries have been making progress over the past two decades, and things were getting better. With the advent of NAFTA, Mexico began generating more jobs, more schools, more universities, more factories, more opportunities. The population explosion in Mexico, which was difficult for an underdeveloped economy to feed, has leveled off due to modern family-planning education and access to birth control. I felt that Mexico could close the wage gap with the U.S. in one more generation, in about another twenty-five years or so. And closing that wage gap would place Mexico in a standing similar to Canada's. Why not build on this progress instead of tearing it apart? Why not keep walking in the same direction?

Consider that before NAFTA, Mexican citizens earned about $1 for every $10 they could earn in the U.S. If your family is in need, and you could swim across the Rio Grande or climb a wall in order to provide a better life for them, wouldn't you? Especially when farmers in the United States are practically begging for workers to help tend the land, because fruit literally rots on trees and leads to the loss of millions in agricultural revenue? It's worth it to note that after only one generation of NAFTA, the wage gap between Mexico and the United States has narrowed by about 50 percent. A person could potentially make $5 in Mexico for every $10 in the U.S.

The possibility of making a living to support one's family lessens the desperation required to risk one's life crossing the border. And despite what has been said about hordes of immigrants sneaking into the U.S., Mexican immigration, legal and illegal, had been steadily dropping even before Trump came into office. The predominant narrative in the United States is that Mexicans are just waiting for the chance to hop over the border, but the truth is that people don't want to leave their home and their family unless they absolutely have to. The ultimate benefit of globalization is domestic stability. The European Union was created not just because those countries wanted to increase their GDPs. The EU was a necessity because interdependent economies meant peace among neighboring nations. What could be better for the United States than to have a southern neighbor as economically vibrant as its northern one? Mexico would be happy to discuss and find solutions for whatever legitimate problems exist with NAFTA's current iteration, but we are not going backward and we are not going to let Trump bully us.

After convincing the world to open its doors, Donald Trump wants the United States to put up walls and close its borders. It's too late for that. The globalization genie is out of the bottle.

Mexico and the rest of the world have seen the Promised Land. The future belongs to interconnectivity and interdependence. I've said this before and I'll say it again: The United States is incredibly important but it is not the world's belly button. China also has a massive economy, second to the United States' and growing bigger every year. If the United States recedes from the world's economic stage, it will leave a space China would be more than happy to fill.

The Western democracies might not agree with China's communist government, but it is no longer a closed-off society, and there has been a rise in advocates for human rights. China has 300 million middle-class people, way more than the United States. It has more infrastructure, airports, and roads brought about through inviolable five-year social and economic development plans. It has an authoritarian system with a relentless discipline that is unfamiliar to both the United States and Mexico. Democracies take time to make decisions and come to terms on laws and policies, and although we don't agree with this strictness, it is what allows China to accomplish so much, so quickly.

Even though China for the most part adheres to the WTO guidelines, it is met with trepidation by the rest of the world because it is such a ferocious competitor. If Trump really wants a monster to scare the U.S. with, he could use China instead of squabbling about milk, tuna, and wood with Canada or Mexico. But fear is counterproductive. China has a population of 1.3 billion people—far greater than Mexico, the U.S., and Canada combined; it is doing what it feels it needs to do to keep all those people fed. The United States is famous for its unfettered capitalism and its strong belief in competition. So why not compete? The smart thing for Trump to do would be to use China's economic ferocity as a way to build a case for why NAFTA should be strengthened, not weakened. Together, we can compete with China on equal footing.

China's relentless productivity is also a reason why the United States should have gone through with the Trans-Pacific Partnership trade agreement. Even if the TPP was not going to be particularly profitable for the U.S. in the immediate term, the idea was to maintain the position of leadership and avail the Americas of all the benefits of partnering and sharing information with other countries.

If Trump turns his back on Mexico, the next-door neighbor who buys more products from the United States than the four largest European nations combined, we will have to look for friends elsewhere. Mexico is on its way to becoming the fifth-largest economy in the world. We love working with and vacationing in the United States, and it is clear that the U.S. loves our food and hospitality and our beaches and beautiful weather. Mexico has plenty of retired Canadian and United States citizens who have realized their dreams of living by the beach. Trump's anti-immigrant sentiments and public insults are damning, and the effects in Mexico are not good—he is kicking a hornet's nest of old-style Mexican nationalism, and that is the last thing he wants in a country that has a large population old enough to harbor a grudge against the invading *"gringos"* and that is sore about lost Mexican territories. If Trump continues to treat us poorly, kick us around, talk to us like we're in the ugly backyard to the south, we have no choice but to look to other countries for business. It will take some work to reorient the logistics of our trading industry, but the Mexican people are strong and proud. We've survived a seventy-year brutal dictatorship and invasions by the Spanish, French, and several by the United States Army. We have a young, dynamic population with a strong work ethic and a burning desire to succeed and pull their families out of poverty. We can sell cars, avocados, computers, and televisions to Europe and China. China, particularly, would be an enormous opportunity for us.

Already, many countries in Latin America, such as Brazil, Argentina, and Chile, have very limited trade with the U.S. but trade very well with China. Mexico hasn't sought a large-scale trade agreement with China yet. We can go further and make agreements with South America and India. The world is bigger than Donald Trump's view of America, and Mexico is much bigger than what Trump has said about our people. We are a successful and cheerful nation; if he doesn't want to work with us, it's his loss. Canada and Mexico are allies, and we'll have each other's backs when Trump wants to renegotiate NAFTA. Of course, I have hope that things will get better—but not because I think Trump himself will change. That man's entire life has been filled with high-powered lawyers and paid sycophants who have made sure he's never had to pay the consequences of his actions and willful ignorance. I do believe, however, that Trump is now trying to play on a whole different field.

The rules of real estate and the rules of public service are quite different. We have already seen that he's not ready for prime time, and this big a spotlight is going to start to burn. The global corporations that are doing so well in Mexico, Canada, and other countries will make themselves heard, and so will the consumers. As United States Republican senator Lindsey Graham tweeted: "Simply put, any policy proposal which drives up costs of Corona, tequila, or margaritas is a big-time bad idea. Mucho Sad."

CHAPTER 2

Immigration:
Racism, Fear of the Other

"We are a country where people of all backgrounds, all nations of origin, all languages, all religions, all races, can make a home. America was built by immigrants."

−Hillary Clinton

I N 1895, A YOUNG American citizen named Joseph Fox from Cincinnati, Ohio, with German and Irish roots, decided to immigrate to what he hoped would be a better place. He was hungry and tired, and ended up in a small, mostly rural town called Guanajuato in Mexico. He settled there in a modest community, married the daughter of a French soldier and an indigenous peasant, and worked his way up from night watchman at a horse carriage factory to the owner of it. He eventually bought a ten-thousand-acre ranch called San Cristobal and started a family. The immigrant's son, José Luis Fox, worked alongside him, and despite losing nine thousand acres during a government takeover in 1938, they expanded it into a thriving enterprise that employed hundreds of fellow Guanajuatans and their families. The immigrant's grandson would go from fellow worker to truck driver to president of Coca-Cola's Mexico division to political advocate and, improbably, president of Mexico.

My grandfather's journey from Ohio to Mexico in search of a better life is the very definition of the American Dream. The same can be said of the journey taken by my maternal grandparents from their native Spain to Mexico at the turn of the twentieth century. Unlike the millions of poor Mexican immigrants who risk their lives to cross the southern border in the hopes of making a better life for their families, I never had the need to move from my home in search of food and opportunity. I came from a family of landowners, extremely hardworking people who were devoutly Catholic. The family had humble beginnings but eventually moved into the upper middle class.

Despite our having a relatively privileged background, my father never let me or my siblings think there was a dollar to spare. I spent my youth waking up at dawn to milk cows, bale hay, and feed the animals right alongside my grandfather, father, and the families who worked for them. I spent the afternoons playing with my siblings and friends, the sons and daughters of the workers. Unlike my friends' parents, my family had the means to send me across the U.S. border to a Jesuit boarding school in Wisconsin at the age of fourteen so I could learn English, though they sent me without a cent in my pocket.

I'd been across the border on only a couple of occasions for short (two-day) trips with my older brother to buy hogs in Texas.

Prior to these trips, we had been insulated from U.S. culture by the xenophobic dictatorship of the PRI political party, which even censored Hollywood films lest the people get too many ideas about "freedom" and "democracy."

It is a terrible feeling to be away from home, in a land where you cannot speak the language. The feeling of isolation is crippling. It was devastating to leave my family and everything I'd known, even if it was for just one year. During that time, I learned English and a few other things, such as U.S.-style racism (Spic. Beaner. Dirty Mexican. "Go back to Mexico." I heard it all). But what really got me was U.S.-style "freedom." To me, it seemed like a magical society where anyone could say anything without fear of being taken away in the middle of the night or losing his or her job. I had to work while going to school, and spent many days bussing tables—I couldn't believe the amount of food that was wasted. Empty Coca-Cola bottles were thrown away without someone collecting the deposit. And everyone, young men and young women, regardless of economic background, went to school.

When I returned home, many of my friends were gone. They'd crossed the border to that magical land on the other side in search of the opportunity that their government denied them. I never forgot them. I realized my privilege only when I saw that my friends had to work instead of going to school, and that they ate mostly tortillas and beans because they couldn't afford meat. Their lives planted the seed of political activism that lay dormant until years later, when I traveled the world as a corporate executive and experienced true democracies at work.

I actually agree with Donald Trump and many others in the United States—the immigration system is broken, and it has to be fixed. But let's keep this in mind: earlier, I said the United States became the richest democracy on earth by convincing others countries to trade. The dark side of the United States' wealth also lies in its exploitation of human beings. Native Americans were forcibly removed from their lands to make way for white settlers, and untold numbers were killed by U.S. military action. Africans were enslaved in the United States for almost three hundred years.

Though slavery was finally abolished in the nineteenth century, it happened only after a bloody civil war, and the effects of segregation and racism are still felt to this very day. Like the abolition of slavery, immigration reform is equal parts a moral question, an economic issue, and a legal matter. Consider that in the "good ol' days" Trump speaks of, during WW II and into the late '60s, the United States signed the Mexican Farm Labor Agreement, by which millions of Mexicans were brought into the U.S. to help fill the shortage of labor when the U.S. soldiers went to fight. These Mexican laborers were promised salaries, decent housing, healthcare, and a savings program. Many of these men, *los braceros*, did not receive the salary, proper healthcare, or savings program they were promised, even though their paychecks showed the deductions. Once they weren't needed anymore, they were sent home, many of them suffering from terrible health problems. Many called this a form of modern slavery.

The program was devastating for future guest-worker partnerships—Mexican nationalists used it as proof that the U.S.

was an imperialist nation of cheaters who couldn't be trusted to keep their word, and U.S. xenophobes decried the flood of immigrants that had lowered the wages of the men coming back from the war.

We don't know exactly how many undocumented immigrants are currently living in the U.S. Estimates are between eleven to fifteen million people, the vast majority of whom are law-abiding, hardworking, decent people who just want to make an honest paycheck and help their family survive back home. Contrary to Trump's racist myths, these people are not here to use government benefits. They are not seeking handouts. They provide a strong labor force for the farming, manufacturing, service, and healthcare industries—they help fund the pensions of retiring United States seniors and provide billions in taxes to the federal and state governments without ever seeing a tax return or a social security check. They are unable to participate in 401(k) plans, and many have no bank account. Imagine if these people were just removed from society. The damage to the economy would be swift and catastrophic; some estimate that the U.S. GDP would drop by almost two trillion dollars. These people are not takers; they are clearly giving everything they have just to survive.

Instead of discussing real ideas on how to bring these people out of the shadows, Donald Trump made deporting people who are in the country illegally a key promise of his campaign. Over and over again, Trump fed his raging crowds visions of Mexican "bad hombres" roaming the streets looking to rob, rape, and kill indiscriminately. He called for a total and complete termination of Muslims' entering the United States, suggested all Muslims should be registered, and declared that "Islam hates us." He told supporters at a rally in Minnesota that Somalis were coming into their neighborhoods without their support or approval, and joining ISIS and spreading radical Islamic views.

Trump repeatedly said the U.S. had no proper vetting system for refugees, when the truth is that refugees have to endure an intense investigative process that takes years to complete. One of the most repulsive things Trump would do at rallies was bring a group of people onstage, mostly women, whom he called "Angel Moms." These women had loved ones who had been murdered by undocumented immigrants. He would then ask each woman to say the name of her loved one, followed by the nationality of the person who had killed that person. It was a disgusting and cruel exploitation of their pain for his anti-immigrant agenda.

The reality is that immigrants (documented or otherwise) are far less likely to commit crimes than citizens. Sadly, these images no doubt cemented the ignorance and bigotry in his supporters' hearts. After being elected, Trump followed through on his promise to create an office just for victims of crimes committed by immigrants who are in the U.S. illegally. In addition to providing "support," the Victims of Immigration Crime Engagement office (VOICE) provides reports of crimes committed by immigrants, a sad reminder of Hitler's Jewish-crime logs that appeared in newspapers, which served to dehumanize and criminalize Jewish people before the "final solution."

A crime is a crime. A victim is a victim. People should call the police. They should have the support of their family and friends and mental health professionals to help overcome the pain of loss. But let's think about this—is the death of a loved one made worse by the fact that the person who caused it was born elsewhere? What if the person who committed the crime is a lawful permanent resident or a naturalized U.S. citizen? Would the victim still get to call VOICE and ask for support services, since the person was born on foreign soil? This is a slippery slope toward a really bad place.

VOICE is a fear-mongering tool, a sham designed to perpetuate stereotypes. What VOICE and the threat of religious registries and mass deportations accomplish is truly sinister—millions of people will become the targets of predators. Undocumented immigrants and people of Muslim faith will be afraid to report being victims of or witnesses to crimes, terrified that they will be removed from their home or placed on a list. These people are already living in the shadows; this would place them in a far darker place. It does not make the United States safer.

The United States' reputation as a melting pot of cultures where all are welcomed at the door by Lady Liberty is fundamental to the moral fabric of the country. The U.S. is, indeed, a nation of immigrants; the American Dream was created and is fueled by those seeking refuge from religious and ethnic persecution. But the United States has an ugly history of keeping certain people out. In the early 1800s the Chinese were vilified as criminals and job takers; the Japanese were excluded in the early 1900s, and then southern and eastern Europeans in the 1920s. Irish Catholics, fleeing a politically induced famine in their country, were considered an inferior race to Anglo-Saxons and encountered discrimination in jobs, housing, and employment. It wasn't until after the horrors of WW II, when the United States turned away

Jewish immigrants desperately fleeing the Nazi regime who later died in concentration camps, that the acceptance of refugees was reframed as a moral obligation. The country made much progress in the hearts and minds of people all over the world as a beacon of hope, the world's richest and most generous democracy. Sadly, that light is dimming with Donald Trump as president. His willful, bigoted misrepresentations have tarnished the modern legacy of inclusion that really does make America great. Consider this—Trump isn't just going after people who were born on foreign soil; he is going after people who were born in the United States. He declared that Mexican American judge Gonzalo Curiel, born in Indiana, would not give him a fair trial in the Trump University fraud case because he was "of Mexican heritage." Trump said the American-born children of Middle Easterners could never really assimilate into American culture and could be "radicalized," and he repeatedly told the lie that he personally saw thousands of Arabs cheering in New Jersey during the terrorist attack on the World Trade Center. For years, Trump peddled conspiracy theories that Barack Obama, the first African American president, was born in Kenya and was a secret Muslim when, in fact, Obama was born in Hawaii and is a Christian. During live Republican debates, Trump questioned Republican candidate Ted Cruz's Cuban heritage and suggested his father may have helped kill John F. Kennedy. He called Democratic senator Elizabeth Warren "the Indian" and "Pocahontas," and accused her of using Native American heritage to further her career.

Trump has given free rein to people who subscribe to racist ideals of white supremacy. Old groups like the Ku Klux Klan had been mostly driven underground but today are holding rallies and finding allies in the modern, sleeker, "alt-right" movements that call for a preservation of white heritage in the United States. These people are dreaming of a whites-only country, and see Trump's promises of mass deportations, religious registries, and travel bans as explicit affirmation of their views. Except the United States has never been a whites-only country. If the country belongs to anyone, it would belong to the Native Americans, who've been here far longer than those first European pioneers. Ethnic- and religious-based hate crimes have skyrocketed under Trump's administration. Children are being bullied more often in school. More Jewish cemeteries have been vandalized, and synagogues have received countless bomb threats. Acts of terrorism worldwide by those who pervert religion also feed into anti-immigrant and race-based fear. And Trump and his cohorts are all too happy to amplify those fears and then offer to save his supporters with bans and walls to keep the scary foreigners out. They know that the fearful find it easier to turn against a fellow human than to organize and turn against a system that keeps them in their place.

Anti-immigrant, "racial purity" sentiments are spreading across the world, with various elections in Europe offering worrying examples. Trump supported presidential hopeful Marine Le Pen in France, whose campaign platform, similarly to Trump's, was about making "France more French," deporting undocumented migrants, and stopping legal migration. In Holland, Geert Wilders (sporting a Trump-like head of hair) promised to remove Holland from the EU, ban all mosques and the Qur'an, and make "the Netherlands for the Netherland people again" because there was "too much Moroccan scum making the streets unsafe." The U.K.'s vote to exit the EU came as a total shock. The "Brexit" campaign was driven by propaganda posters showing hordes of immigrants and the slogan "Take Back Our Borders." Knowing the horrors of WW II, it was demoralizing to hear the rise of ethnocentrism in the European Union from countries that had seen more than seventy years of peace. Thankfully, the people of France and Holland chose to vote against the message of hate and fear. The U.K. is clearly having buyer's remorse about its choice to exit the EU, since a 40 percent voter share in the last general election went to Jeremy Corbyn, of the opposition Labour Party, who believes in bridges, not walls.

This fear that somehow cultures are being erased or diluted by immigrants is a false one. We need only look at thousands of years of world history to see that far from being diluted, the best aspects of each culture are strengthened when they come into contact with one another. What survives the passing of time, what gets handed down from person to person, generation to generation, regardless of location, are the values, cuisine, art, and language that are strong, that are real. Mexicans didn't stop making the best tequila on earth because we "globalized." We didn't stop making traditional Mexican coffee because Starbucks came to Mexico, or stop making delicious tacos because we could also eat at McDonald's. In fact, McDonald's tweaks its menu to suit the tastes of people in all parts of the world. The place where cultures meet just makes things more interesting, more vibrant, and people have choices. Those who call for a return to "racial purity" and "the good ol' days" are peddling fake dreams to the intellectually lazy, morally corrupt, and spiritually destitute.

Immigration is America's greatest asset. Immigrants are actually the first and most ardent patriots, because having fled poverty, the ravages of war, brutal dictatorships, and general lawlessness, they know how precious, how extraordinary, "the American experiment" truly is. And they spread that love of country, that belief in the American Dream and the ideals of democracy and equality to their birth land when they visit their families. In 2016, all six of America's Nobel Prize winners were immigrants. These people have brought their talents to the United States and work tirelessly to make incredible discoveries that will continue to cement the United States' position as the Leader of the Free World.

Immigrants keep the country young and dynamic. I agree that we need comprehensive immigration reform in order to fix what is clearly a broken system. You can't have almost fifteen million people in the shadows, without access to proper healthcare, education, any kind of representation in society. Demonizing, dehumanizing, and deporting immigrants is not the way. During my political years, I found many a sympathetic ear within both the Democratic and Republican parties about the issue of Mexican immigration, but real action was hard to get through the deliberative bodies. Usually one side wanted the focus to be on securing the border, while the other side's focus was on the civil rights of the immigrants. But George W. Bush and I were kindred spirits.

I first met George W. Bush in 1996 when he was governor of Texas and I was governor of my home state of Guanajuato. I tried and failed to pitch him a Marshall-like plan between our states. Four years later, we both became presidents of our countries. He honored Mexico by making it his first international visit, and I took the opportunity to try to pitch him again. I was determined to do what I could for the Mexicans working in the United States and struggling to survive, and improve the standard of life for all Mexicans so they would not feel obligated to leave. Bush also shared the view that something had to be done for the millions who were contributing to America from the shadows but had no basic rights. He also understood that Latinos were a key swing vote in U.S. elections—given the Republicans' "traditional family values" brand, their message would be incredibly appealing to Latinos who are of deep faith and believe in the importance of family. If the Republicans weren't so busy insulting the integrity of Mexican immigrants, they would have a powerful ally in their elections.

President Bush and I agreed on a NAFTA Plus-type program that expanded the relationship between our countries beyond the trade of goods—it detailed a plan for shared responsibility for border security, combatting crime and illegal migration, as well as improving the lives of those who were already living and working in the U.S. Most important, we agreed that NAFTA Plus would have an educational component, a sort of intellectual exchange program by which we would get educational institutions involved in the sharing of ideas on technology, science, and the eradication of poverty.

We both knew that the way to address illegal immigration was by giving desperate people a reason to stay home. Canada shares a border with the U.S., but you don't see many Canadians sneaking over it. This is because there is no reason to. The standard of living is similar. But this kind of economic parity takes time, innovation, and perseverance. The idea was to approach the complex immigration issue with a clear mind, compassion, and a sound economic rationale. The basic tenets of the plan to address the undocumented workers in the U.S. were:

1. Anyone who could prove that he or she was actively working in the United States would get legal status. This would be different from becoming a United States citizen or a lawful permanent resident. These legal workers would have to continue proving employment status on a yearly or biannual basis. If they couldn't prove it, they would have to return to Mexico.

2. Offer a status adjustment process for those who ultimately wanted to become citizens. Becoming a citizen is a personal decision. To the surprise of many, becoming a U.S. citizen is not the predominant desire of Latinos who cross the border. They come only to work and support their families and dream of going back home when things get better. But those who fall in love with the United States, who put down roots and want to contribute to the democratic experiment, should have a real path to citizenship.

3. Create a comprehensive guest-worker program for future migrant workers that would apply history's lessons of past failures and successes. A certain number of workers with proven places to work would be allowed in, and the

total number of yearly participants would fluctuate with the country's GDP.

It wasn't perfect, but I was thrilled with the idea that millions of people would be immediately helped by the proposed plan. President Bush promised to sell it to the right-wing faction of his party, and I was invited speak at a joint meeting of Congress about U.S.-Mexico relations on September 6, 2001. I spoke about the two countries' long and complicated history and the need for trust, given that our destinies would forever be tied together by geography. I was given a standing ovation, and there was nothing but hope in my heart. But the hope would not last. On September 11, 2001, one of the most horrific acts of terror we have ever experienced effectively ended any discussions about comprehensive immigration reform, and the country shut down its borders and started to build walls.

Almost two decades later, we have not gotten much further. Studies show that the majority of Americans favor a comprehensive immigration policy. If Donald Trump really wants to drain the swamp and shake things up, he should go get the plan George W. Bush and I agreed on, dust it off, and take credit for it. He should use his great negotiating skills to get it passed into law. He likes putting his name on things he didn't work on. I wouldn't mind this at all.

CHAPTER 3

The Wall

"My hand will be against the prophets who see false visions and utter lying divinations.... They have misled My people by saying, 'Peace!' when there is no peace. And when anyone builds a wall... I will tear down the wall which you plastered over with whitewash and bring it down to the ground, so that its foundation is laid bare; and when it falls, you will be consumed in its midst. And you will know that I am the Lord."

—Ezekiel 13:10-16

IN 1987, MIRED IN the Cold War conflict with the nuclear-powered Soviet Union, Ronald Reagan won the hearts of many during a speech in which he told Mikhail Gorbachev to "tear down this wall." Today, Donald Trump has ascended to the presidency by selling dreams to his supporters of a "tall," "beautiful," "impenetrable" wall on the border with Mexico. And he promised Mexico would pay for it. It is truly saddening to hear the leader of a country that convinced the world to open its markets, a country made strong by people from all over the world, seriously discussing building a racist monument.

I was a rather average student, but I loved history. I couldn't get enough of reading the stories of Mexico's struggle for independence and freedom, the wars of Napoleon and Genghis Khan, George Washington and the American Revolution. And if we are to learn history's lesson, it is this: walls are useless. The Great Wall of China didn't work, the Berlin Wall fell, and the West Bank barrier has served only to harden hearts and fuel extremist violence, not bring about peace. They all come crashing down in the end. Why? Because there is something in each of us that compels us to come together. It is our nature, even when born into our respective tribes, to seek adventure and form new relationships, new partnerships.

What good are walls now when airplanes and drones can fly over them? When television and the internet show us what is on the other side? And where there are no airplanes or televisions or internet, people can get very creative—homemade bombs put holes in walls; those seeking refuge and to be reunited with their families tunnel under walls, risk their lives on barbed wire to get over those walls. For Americans especially, the idea of walls is anathema to the spirit of the country. The United States is all about the freedom of its citizens to move about as they choose. But after the horrific evil that was 9/11, the country became gripped in fear and the only answers seemed to be a physical barrier with its neighbor, tougher penalties on employers who hired undocumented workers, and the criminalization of undocumented migration. Gone were any considerations of guest-worker programs, much less a path to citizenship.

THE WALL

The border between the United States and Mexico is roughly around two thousand miles long along four states from California to Texas. Half of the border is along the Colorado River and the Rio Grande—vast stretches of desert land and other difficult terrain. Right now, there are about seven hundred miles of border with a combination of wall and fencing built according to President Bush's Secure Fence Act of 2006, which he said to me was just the first step toward a broader comprehensive immigration reform sometime in the future.

The wall was supposed to stop the flow of drugs and illegal migrants and prevent another act of terrorism on U.S. soil. The problem is that it hasn't stopped or even slowed the flow of drugs or illegal migrants, and it hasn't prevented any act of terrorism because no terrorist has ever traveled across the border—religious extremists come in on airplanes, and they are also born and made in the USA (and they come in all shapes and sizes and colors). As it stands, the seven-hundred-mile wall has been a waste of billions of taxpayer dollars and an eyesore for both U.S. and Mexican citizens who live near the border.

The wall rekindled anti-USA sentiment in Mexico, with the nationalists pointing to its building as yet more proof that there was really no true friendship between the countries. With all the technology available to us today and all of the access the United States has to the brightest minds, the best Trump can come up with to secure the safety of the American people is a wall? How are you going to build a wall across rivers? Across desert sand and mountains? What about the devastation to the environment? What about the wild animals that live in or around the border, whose migration patterns have already been disrupted and will die of thirst and starvation? The plan is lunacy.

Politicians, economists, and private-sector professionals know the truth—the wall is a waste of time, money, and energy. But politicians in all parties make deals to quiet their constituents suffering from economic anxiety in order to stay in power, enacting laws that don't offer long-term solutions. Besides, we all know that when the funds run low, and cost-cutting measures are implemented, it will be Mexicans and other Latin Americans standing out in the sun digging and pouring concrete.

The people of the United States are bombarded with images of migrants illegally crossing the border carrying bags full of drugs, and of violent shootouts and dismemberments by competing drug gangs in Mexico, along with stories of rampant corruption in government and overall anarchy in the streets. While gratuitous, those images and stories are real, and in order to grasp the problem in its entirety, the public also has to know that the drug trade is an estimated $30-billion-dollar-a-year, highly sophisticated market, paid for by the insatiable demand for drugs in the United States. Both countries have partnered to fight the drug cartels but, just like with religious extremism, we are up against an enemy that cannot be stopped by a wall. Because the wall won't stop the actual root of the problem— people want to use drugs and, since drugs are illegal, the cartels are the supplier.

The United States is the biggest consumer of drugs in the entire world. It is also the biggest supplier of guns directly used by the Mexican cartels. Over two hundred thousand youths working for the cartels have been killed in the streets, either by the cartels themselves or during the clashes between cartels and Mexican officials. Thousands of police officers, military members, judges, lawyers, and journalists have also been killed. All of these promising lives have been extinguished due to a decades-long drug war. Where bribes don't work, the cartels turn to kidnapping and other forms of crimes to make people complicit.

During my presidency from 2000 to 2006, my administration did everything it could to stem the corruption and violence that had sprung from the decades-long drug trade but, ultimately, we did not do as well as I'd hoped. Mexico was a new real democracy with a still-emerging economy, and we had to balance the need for peace, education, and job creation with an all-out war that I knew had taken many lives. Sadly, in 2006, the next Mexican president, Felipe Calderón, escalated the military's role in the drug war. The military was not prepared to deal with criminals in the way that law enforcement is trained to work in tandem with the judicial body. This led to deadly and unnecessary violence. In addition to this, a major unforeseen side effect of getting the military involved in the drug war was exposure to corruption within their ranks by the cartels.

The biggest problem when anyone comes up against the cartels is money. The drug trade is a global enterprise working with vast amounts of capital. In a developing country, money is king. The cartels are able to recruit thousands of youths and government officials to help keep the trade alive and well. Let's imagine young people with dreams of getting an education and a good-paying job so they can help take care of their family. Just as I realized the difference between my being able to go to school while my friends could not, these youths become conscious of the fact that there are few options except crossing the border. But, before they cross the border to make $10 per hour, a member of a cartel offers them $20. That's $20 more than nothing, and they won't have to cross the border and risk their lives. It is the same with a police officer or a judge, who can make an entire year's salary by taking just one bribe.

I completely agree that we have a serious crime and drug problem, but the problem has to be seen with clear eyes. The Mexican cartels didn't create the drug problem in the United States; they provide the routes through which these drugs get to the border. The major producers of cocaine are Colombia, Venezuela, Ecuador, and Bolivia. Sadly, the opioid-addiction epidemic in the United States has also fueled opium production in southern Mexico. When you hear politicians shrieking that Mexico is bringing drugs and crime into the United States, remember that the only reason the drugs are coming is because Americans wants to buy.

Mexico is caught between a rock and a hard place—drugs are flowing in from our southern border with Central and South America, and guns are flowing in from our northern border with the United States. The relatively lax gun laws in the U.S. make it possible for the cartels to purchase weapons used to defend their territory and line the streets with blood. The wall isn't going to stop the desire for drugs or cure the illness that is addiction. This can be done only with comprehensive healthcare, drug, and gun control reform.

No one knows how much Donald Trump's impenetrable wall would actually cost—but it is estimated that we are talking about

$25 billion to $40 billion just for building it. After this, many more billions would go into the maintenance. Imagine what the United States could do with that money—pay 50,000 teachers for a decade, fund a college education for 250,000 students, fund programs that would rehabilitate drug abusers, and launch national educational efforts about drug use. As the Leader of the Free World, the U.S. could also use the money for three years' worth of clean drinking water for the entire globe or one entire year without world hunger; it could fund disease research that would protect us from a global plague. Or the U.S. could put that money in a revolving, Marshall Plan-like fund with Mexico that could generate five million jobs in Mexico, and particularly promote development in southern Mexico, where the majority of indigenous people live and where desperate migrants from Central and South America first come and then make their way to the northern border with the United States.

As Colombian president Juan Manuel Santos said, "The best wall you can build is economic development.... The strategic interests of the United States are in Latin America...look to the south. If you see that, then you won't need walls." Why doesn't Trump, with his big ideas and negotiating skills, just sit down with Latin American representatives of government and leaders in technology and information industries and discuss plans that can be put in place to generate employment and opportunity?

Over the past thirty years, Mexico has promoted economic development programs that we'd hoped would stop so many from risking their lives on the border, such as the *maquiladoras*, or manufacturing operations built along the U.S.-Mexico border. There are three and a half million workers, assembling things like television screens, computer parts, and automobiles for companies from all over the world. The factories employ millions of people who might have crossed illegally if the work didn't exist. Mexico has over fifty thousand immigrants from varying countries in Latin America working in the booming Mexican coffee fields alone.

There are many labor activists who criticize the lack of workers' rights at the *maquiladoras*, but there are efforts to improve conditions. However, walls are not going to fix the socioeconomic issues that force people to move from their homes. Mexico still has an emerging economy, and though we have made great strides in the past twenty years, we have quite a way to go in order to raise the standard of living for all of our citizens. The fact that illegal immigration continued to decline and wages were going up showed we were on the right path. Trump's "Mexico will pay for the wall" was a hurtful and callous insult because it ignores our valiant struggle and the lives we have lost in partnering with the U.S. to stop the drug trade. Of course, to the surprise of no one who follows politics, Trump went from "Mexico will pay" to the taxpayers would pay first and then Mexico would pay it back…eventually.

Trump also proposed a border tax to fund the wall, and increased visa fees to Mexicans visiting the United States, and finally threatened to halt or tax remittances from hardworking immigrants to their families. Mexico receives about $25 billion from its hardworking citizens in the United States—more than the oil-export industry and more than the tourism industry. It is an incredibly important, vital part of the Mexican economy.

There are those who say that remittances represent money being bled from the U.S. economy, but that is completely false. As I have said, immigrants are contributing far more to the U.S. economy than they are getting back, and the remittance companies already subject customers to significant handling fees. This money helps their families back home so they, too, don't have to cross the border out of desperation. There is something morally and ethically corrupt in any effort to stop working people from sending money back to their families, money they earned with their blood, sweat, and tears.

I believe in borders, and I believe in the law. But I also believe that borders and the law do not mean that we then throw reason, logic, truth, justice, and compassion out the window. In the case of illegal immigration, the wall would make it harder for some to cross, but not impossible for all. And the fact is that almost half of undocumented immigrants in the United States came over on a plane and overstayed their visa. Donald Trump's "wall in the sky" Muslim ban will try to stop this, but a nation founded on law and religious freedom will destroy this ban in the Supreme Court.

In the case of the drug trade, as long as there is a demand for drugs, there will be a supply and all of the violence that accompanies it. We should tackle the drug problem both by decriminalizing drug use so that cartels and dealers lose their power, and promoting education about the effects of drugs. In other words, just like with smoking and alcohol, shift the burden of regulation to the people—it has to be about personal responsibility. The wall wouldn't fix anything in the long run. It would be just a racist monument in the political theater—a physical manifestation of Trump's perverted never-has-been fantasy of Eurocentric whiteness as "American purity."

Trump and his followers think that somehow, if the Africans, Latinos, Arabs, Indians, Asians, and so on are kicked out of the country, America will return to its past grandeur. But America's grandeur was created by immigration—people of every shade, from every part of the world, coming together and becoming one. That is what makes "the American experiment" so special. Trump has stained the U.S. with his talk of Muslim bans and walls, confirming the worst suspicions of anti-American ideologues working hard to subvert their own countries' steps toward more liberal democracies. Trump and his cohorts have perverted the United States' reputation as one built in the spirit of cooperation, equality, and justice.

Already, tourism to the United States is down. Already, the best and brightest minds, both in and outside the United States, yearning for the opportunity to unleash their talents, are turning their sights to Canada, France, and Germany—countries whose recent elections have shown the triumph of the people over hatred and bigotry.

Walls are for the fearful. You do not start building walls in the Land of the Free. The United States doesn't keep its people behind concrete and barbed wire. Consider the miracle of the European Union, twenty-eight countries, all of diverse backgrounds, speaking different languages, all bound by shared policies on trade, banking, currency, environment, security, education, and free travel between them for its citizens— basically, a one-for-all set of values and laws. Instead of walls after WW II, the wealthiest members, like England, Germany, and France, contributed a larger percentage of their GDP to promote investment, education, and infrastructure in their less developed neighbors, like Ireland, Spain, Portugal, Greece, Poland, Hungary, and Czechoslovakia. Because of the European Union, the less wealthy countries increased from $3,000 per capita to more than $30,000 today.

We cannot forget that the United States helped the European Union become a reality with the Marshall Plan. I choose to hold onto this as the true legacy of the United States—a country that helped end the war and helped forge true peace among neighbors. I choose to believe in this "grand experiment," this vibrant multidimensional mosaic of people from everywhere in the world coming together, each striving for a better life and a better world. *E pluribus unum*—out of many, one. This dream of unified plurality is what I'd hoped to accomplish when I tried to convince President Bush and other U.S. leaders of my own dream of a NAFTA Plus union shaped in a style similar to the European one.

As president, I was caught in a political firestorm and considered a traitor by Mexican nationalists for my desire to bring Mexico closer to the United States. Despite the sharp criticism from Mexican and other Latino leaders, I remain convinced this is the way forward. Globalization is here to stay, but the liberal democracies need to find ways to improve on the machinations of this world economy so that it works better for everyone, not just the wealthiest. And I believe we need to start with our neighbors. I dream of a NAFTA Plus that with time will eventually become a SuperNAFTA—where the economies of both the North and South American continents are joined into a strong American Common Market. Imagine that. Together we are over one billion strong, and there is no limit to what we could accomplish if we helped each other, if we made it easier to share ideas, goods and services.

In 1963, John F. Kennedy gave a speech in West Berlin in which he affirmed the United States' commitment to defend Germany against Soviet communist aggression. He said, "Freedom has many difficulties and democracy is not perfect, but we have never had to put a wall up to keep our people in." That was the United States people knew and loved the world over, the country that came to the aid of an ailing one, spreading the message of peace, prosperity, and liberation from tyranny. It is true—freedom does have a price and democracy is guaranteed only in the people's will to continue striving toward a more perfect union. I believe the price of freedom is worth it, and I trust that President Abraham Lincoln's "better angels of our nature" will keep us moving forward.

PART 2

THE CHALLENGES WE FACE

Climate Change and the Environment, Healthcare and Welfare, Women and Education

CHAPTER 4

Climate Change and the Environment

"Some scientists believe climate change is the cause of unprecedented melting of the North Pole... I think we should listen to those scientists and experts."

—THE DALAI LAMA

DONALD TRUMP SEEMS PATHOLOGICALLY obsessed with "national security" and has vowed to increase defense spending along with cracking down on an imagined hostile immigrant takeover. Yet, for all of Trump's mania about increasing military might and hiring thousands of new customs and border patrol officers, he doesn't understand that physical walls and Muslim travel bans cannot protect anyone from the single biggest threat humanity faces today. Climate change is real, its effects are getting ever more dramatic, and the world as we know it faces an existential crisis unless we all work together to slow down and reverse it.

I was raised on a ranch where our very lives depended on the land and the animals. When you grow up so close to the land, you tune in to the cycle of life—the air, the rain, the clouds, the animals…you cannot help but have a deep, reverential respect for the environment and for all living creatures. Everything we need to live—the water we drink, the air we breathe, the food we grow and hunt, the shelter we build, and the clothes we wear—every single thing we need is provided by this earth. We are utterly dependent on the environment, and this is precisely why we need to take care of it.

The overwhelming majority of the scientific community has agreed that climate change is real and that humans are directly contributing to the earth's warming. Trump, however, is on record absurdly saying climate change is a hoax perpetrated by the Chinese in order to gain economic leverage over the United States. Again, his attacks on another country are based on xenophobic propaganda—he asks that his constituents deny the reality of widely accepted, evidence-based, scientific data because the "alternative fact" is that foreigners want to bring harm to the United States.

It is hard to know whether Trump actually believes his own propaganda, or whether he is speaking from political expediency to rile up his 30 percent base of supporters, but ask anyone who has lived as long as Trump and I both have, anywhere in the world, and that person will tell you the climate is changing, because we can see it with our own eyes. A vivid example for me is the Lerma River, which travels to my home state of Guanajuato from the state of Toluca. I saw this river go from being a pristine, almost 500-mile-long body of water that provided water for millions of people to today having just 10 percent of its former capacity.

When I was running for president of Mexico, it was of extreme importance to me that Mother Earth be at the top of the political agenda for the first time in my country's history. I won the presidency with a coalition of special interests that included the Green Party. My ultimate goal, of course, was to help bring Mexico into a democratic, fiscally prosperous future, but it was my firm belief that the country's economic development had to be tied in with absolute respect for the environment. During my travels all over my country, I'd seen indigenous communities who lived off the natural environment and who depended on it for nourishment and housing, have to make do with the remnants of what rampant industrial development had left—scorched lands and polluted rivers. I knew that we needed to make use of Mexico's vast natural resources to improve the country's wealth, but we also had to protect the untouched land we had left and clean up that which we had directly destroyed.

Humanity's needs obviously have a direct impact on the environment—we are causing massive disruptions in the balance of wildlife by overfishing and overhunting; we are polluting the quality of our air and water by burning fossil fuels, and changing the composition of our land with agricultural practices that eventually lead to desertification of once fertile earth. While our very own direct actions impact our immediate environment, the more consequential threat is what our actions are causing on a global scale.

Science has shown that climate change is caused by the release of carbon dioxide, as a direct consequence of burning fossil fuels for our energy needs. We need to move from fossil fuels to other forms of energy as soon as possible, and we need to increase the efficiency of our current energy use. If we don't change our ways, the future of all living things looks dire. Climate change is already the leading cause of mass animal and human migrations, which lead to intensifying conflicts as people fight for diminished resources. The resulting displacement and dislocation cause cracks in the social cohesion necessary for domestic political stability. Rising sea levels, floods, droughts, and heat waves are all natural events that force migration.

Many articles have been written about the direct consequences of climate change on geopolitics. For example, after years of study, experts have now drawn a direct connection between the horrifying war in Syria and the region's worst drought in almost one thousand years. The drought caused 75 percent of the farmlands along with the majority of the livestock to be destroyed. Millions of people of varying tribes and factions in Syria were displaced and forced together into limited territory because of a lack of food and water.

A fight for resources lowers the capacity for tolerance and understanding between people and exacerbates political strife and chaos; this is especially true in tribal-based cultures. Even the U.S. Pentagon recognizes that global warming is a strategic threat to political stability the world over—with infrastructure destroyed and limited access to food and water, disease spreads and people have to choose between leaving or certain death. Geopolitical upheaval also breeds and spreads extremist ideologies among a desperate population looking for immediate help and answers.

Despite the years of research and the evidence we have available, the world is still divided on how to counter global climate change. We have plenty of solutions, but there remains a debate on specific methods and whether the industrialized nations should bear the majority of the cost. For example, Mexico has made a rapid and widespread social, political, and economic transformation over the past two decades, but compared to the United States, it is still a developing nation. In an emerging market, people want solutions to poverty in the here and now. Those who are very poor have needs that are immediate—they are not thinking about protecting the land for their children's children; they are thinking of their next meal.

My administration's struggle to negotiate economic growth with environmental responsibility in mind did not come without a fight—there were farmers who resisted the government trying to put an end to slash-and-burn agriculture or our attempts to enact policies that would revert farmland back to protected status. There were many times that environmental protection actions were met with violence from Mexican citizens, as men wielded machetes to protect their traditional rights to burn forests, cut down trees, or poison lakes and rivers with banned pesticides that helped keep their crops from illness but were making people sick. Every sweeping change we made in the hopes of bettering life for everyone directly impacted some people in a way that they found unfair.

Change is always painful, especially for those who don't have much to begin with. There will be those who appear, at first, to lose out immediately—people who will no longer be able to farm as they want and people who will lose jobs in industries that are no longer able to meet certain environmental regulations, but it the job of leaders to find ways to help them thrive, not lie to them.

Similar to the agricultural "losers" in Mexico's fight for environmental health, the United States faces a challenge with the coal industry, seen by many rural states as part of the very fabric of their community. Once a thriving industry that paid its hardworking men and women a relatively good salary, coal is fast becoming obsolete due to natural gas, cheaper renewable energies, and environmental regulations. Coal is now a symbol of bygone days—an industry more closely associated with industrial pollution and the contamination of the human body. In addition, what's left of the coal industry will soon be completely taken over by automation.

Hillary Clinton attempted what many politicians still don't—she was honest about the declining industry and put forth plans to retrain workers who had already been laid off and those who would be in the future. Despite the data and the science about the dangers of coal, Donald Trump exploited the miners by promising to revive the industry and put them back to work. Instead of honesty, Trump offered a time machine to the past; sadly, enough people believed him. The stark reality is that the energy industry is moving away from fossil fuels and toward solar, wind, and other renewable energy alternatives.

As the wealthiest and most progressive country, the United States should be leading the charge in innovative energy technology. Instead, Trump's administration is peddling lies and misinformation. Right now, the United States has almost three times as many jobs in the solar industry as it does in coal. Trump's promises to "bring back the coal industry" are misleading because he cannot stop the forward progress of time or the invisible hand of the market. There is a global movement toward sustainable, efficient energy production—all Trump can try to do is delay it, at great cost to the people of his country in terms of both their health and their immediate environmental surroundings, when he should be looking for viable paths for their economic future.

When I was president, I strongly admired countries like Ireland, New Zealand, Canada, and Costa Rica, who had made great economic progress while also protecting their natural assets and creating booming ecotourism industries. During my administration, we followed their examples and declared that about four million acres of Mexican jungle, mountains, deserts, and marshlands would be left untouched by developers. Our hope was that the indigenous people living in those villages would someday benefit from the same profitable ecotourism that Costa Rica does. The money generated from visitors would help create jobs, bring in money that could be used for education, and help lift the people out of poverty.

Mexico also worked with the United States in creating the North American Development Bank, a binational financial institution, as part of the NAFTA agreement. The NADBank both invested in and directly funded environmentally sound infrastructure projects and provided clean water for those who lived near the border, where the majority of global industries were located. While I never did get the Marshall-style, EU-like plan between Mexico and the United States I'd pitched to George Bush when I was governor and later president, the NADBank had the same spirit.

Despite the antiglobalist attitudes of many in my own country, it was the global corporations that brought their already strict regulation policies along with them, and we were able to gain quite a bit of knowledge about the best practices to maintain environmental health. Today, we are at a perilous moment in humanity's existence, and bi-national agreements and partnerships are not enough to save us. We ultimately need to come together as a planet in order to have a substantial effect on our planet. We must remember that the earth is sacred—it does not belong to us; it belongs to God. What will it matter if we reap all the riches, if we destroy our home in the process?

This coming together of the global community is what we ultimately hope to accomplish with the Paris climate accord, led by the U.S. and China, the world's two largest economies and polluters. The accord is sponsored by the United Nations, and it is a pact among every country to adopt more green energy sources and cut down on greenhouse gas emissions in an effort to limit the global temperature increase to no more than 2 degrees Celsius above preindustrial levels. The agreement requires transparency between nations and encourages sharing climate data. There is also a Green Climate Fund, to which developed nations will contribute in order to help less industrialized nations adapt to environmentally healthy practices and mitigate their losses in doing so.

After my presidency was over, I was overjoyed to see Mexico's leaders continue along the path toward environmental health and enthusiastically sign on to the Paris climate accord. There are only two countries that have not signed the agreement. Nicaragua, still a developing nation, argues that the richer nations should actually be paying even more into the green fund, because they are causing more of the climate change. Syria is sadly mired in a horrific war. Nicaragua's argument that the agreement doesn't go far enough and Syria's inability to sign serve to highlight the utter dereliction of duty in Trump's decision to remove the United States from the agreement.

I have to say that I, along with the most of the rest of the world, see Trump's decision to renege on this most imperative global project as bizarre and just completely incomprehensible. Trump stopped saying that climate change was a con and a hoax once he got elected—many hoped he would come around once he was briefed on classified government data. Instead, Trump called a press briefing on the White House lawn and made a pompous speech in which he pitted the United States against the entire world. Instead of discussing just China's taking advantage of the United States, Trump presented a globalized version of his climate conspiracy theory—this time, the Paris accord was nothing but an attempt by other nations to use the United States as a piggy bank.

"At which point does America get laughed at?" he asked, before going on to assert that signing on to the agreement would cause American workers to lose their jobs. In a nod to his "America first" policy, he said that he had been "elected to represent the citizens of Pittsburgh, not Paris." Of course, the problem is that both Pittsburgh and Paris are on planet Earth. The effort to combat climate change has to be a global one, and Trump's shortsightedness and unwillingness to join the effort based on his failed business policies will serve only to diminish his beloved country's lead on the sustainable energy revolution and the millions of new jobs and technological advances that will come from it.

Despite whatever Trump says, we know the future is green. Trump's ignorance and inability to think outside of his immediate circumstances make him color-blind. Even before his announcement about the Paris climate accord, Trump began his administration with a slew of executive orders aimed at removing President Obama's environmental regulations on energy industries that were meant to protect land, air, and water. He also removed edicts that required companies to consider the latest findings on climate science data when planning infrastructure projects. Trump's federal budget proposed steep cuts to scientific research and programs aimed at curbing pollution and waste. Most significantly, Trump has appointed a slew of climate change deniers and skeptics, as well as fossil fuel tycoons, to his cabinet, clearly displaying his intention to place short-term economic growth ahead of environmental health.

Nevertheless, the people of the United States will take on the fight for the planet's health. Thankfully, legislators on both the city and state levels across the United States are openly defying Donald Trump's shortsightedness and vowing to follow emissions guidelines along with the rest of the world in the Paris climate accord. I have faith that those who love the earth and understand the peril will outlast Trump, but his effect on general attitudes about environmental protections and regulations is real and chilling.

In addition to immediate adverse effects on the land, air, and water of the United States, there might just be an American brain drain. Emmanuel Macron, the young, charismatic new president of France, openly called for American environmental scientists to come to France since it was clear the Trump administration did not respect their work. In a direct affront to Trump's embarrassingly nationalist "America first" vision, Macron stood on a world stage and asked that we all come together to "make our planet great again." It is truly hard to believe just how much the image of the United States as world leader has been tarnished. The same country that came to prominence by attracting talent from all over the world may now begin to lose those great minds because of Trump's demagoguery.

The sad truth is that despite the fact that the United States is a country of great wealth, people like Trump and those he surrounds himself with are motivated mainly by greed, by how much they can get in the here and now. The earth may have enough resources to sustain life for thousands or millions more years, but not if we don't respect it. World-renowned scientist Stephen Hawking has made it very clear that we're at an incredibly precarious point in time and if we don't act now, the changes to Mother Earth will be irreversible. Hawking asserted that, "by denying the evidence for climate change, and pulling out of the Paris Climate Agreement, Trump will cause avoidable environmental damage to our beautiful planet, endangering the natural world, for us and our children."

If we are to save our planet, we must listen to those who have dedicated their lives to science and to the pursuit of truth. We need to spread the message of climate change and environmental responsibility far and wide. We need to work incessantly to remove the skepticism about global warming from public discourse. As I write this, a massive one-trillion-ton iceberg has broken off the ice cap in Antarctica. The icebergs are melting, causing sea levels to rise at a faster rate than ever before. Soon, landmasses that are now just above sea level will be completely uninhabitable. Humans cannot live underwater, and we cannot live without water. We cannot waste our breath discussing whether global warming is actually happening. We are running out of time.

CHAPTER 5

Healthcare and Welfare

"The moral test of government is how that government treats those who are in the dawn of life, the children; those who are in the twilight of life, the elderly; those who are in the shadows of life, the sick, the needy and the handicapped."

—HUBERT HUMPHREY, former vice president
of the United States

THERE IS A FAMOUS parable that exists in many religions both of the East and the West. The parable is about heaven and hell—the circumstances and tools are different depending on the teller, but the message is always the same. A student asks a wise person what the difference is between heaven and hell. The student is first shown a place where the people are sitting around a table laden with almost every food imaginable. Despite the abundance of food, the people are skeletal and starving. They have long spoons tied to their hands and are unable to bend their arms, so they cannot bring the long spoons to their mouths. It is a scene of absolute horror and abject misery. That is hell.

The student is then shown another scene where people are sitting around a similar table equally laden with food, but here the people are happy and well fed. They, too, are unable to bend their arms and have long spoons tied to their hands. The student cannot understand why both groups have the same amount of food and the same tools but their condition is so different. The wise person explains that in hell the people are trying to feed themselves, but in heaven the people know to feed each other.

The exact origins of this story are unknown, but what is remarkable is that it is a nearly universal tale of the need for shared responsibility. The core of the message is that we simply cannot go it alone. In order to survive, humans need to help one another. As the world moves closer together, it becomes harder and harder to turn our back on our neighbors who are less fortunate than we are. I believe there has to be a massive, urgent, renewed emphasis on the teaching of compassion, empathy, and human unity.

Around the world, one-third of all food is thrown away. In the United States, almost 50 percent of produce is thrown away or allowed to rot because of blemishes that do not affect the taste or nutrient content. If we can throw away so much food, then how is it possible that millions of people around the world are hungry? Research has shown that today we have the scientific and technological prowess to feed every single person on earth. Tragically, droughts and floods that cause crop failures are acts of nature, but actual famine is human-made. There are people who are systematically starving to death not because there is no food, but because their governments have failed and oftentimes warring political factions prevent foreign aid from getting to the people. Tyrannical governments have historically used hunger as a weapon to bend the citizenry to their will. We must have a resurgence of compassion, a renewed sense of the connection between humans, communities, and nations. We must dedicate resources to those who are actively working in the fields of economics, science, and technology—these minds that will figure out how best to get resources where they are needed.

The United States is the richest country on earth based on GDP, yet ranks second to last of developed countries in terms of the percentage of foreign aid money that goes to alleviating poverty and disease, and assisting disaster relief and environmental efforts, in the rest of the world. It is a little-known fact that U.S. citizens, corporations, and charities actually give more to those in need than the U.S. government. This is why Donald Trump standing on the world stage during the NATO summit crowing about other countries' paying their "fair share" of anything is particularly galling. The European Union and Japan, both brought back from the brink of extinction by the Marshall Plan, actually give a higher percentage of their GDP for foreign aid than America does.

We can all agree that you cannot have a functioning global or domestic democracy without laws that dictate behavior, but I would also argue that you cannot have a stable world order when there are people who are literally starving and have nowhere to turn in times of need. The best border security that the United States can hope for is stability in the democratic image that it has convinced the rest of the world can work. Trump's election has given everyone serious cause for concern. Already, Trump has planned to cut foreign aid to the poorest regions of Africa—regions most in danger of famine, war, and extremist ideological recruiting.

I'm not saying the United States is responsible for fixing everybody else's problems, but I am saying the country that has so greatly benefitted from open trade should consider this when looking at poverty elsewhere. Wouldn't it make better sense to help starving people in Somalia than to execute a stupid wall plan on the southern border with Mexico? Research has shown that U.S.-funded global health research initiatives not only bring about medical innovations that save millions of lives abroad and at home, but they also create jobs and bring investments to the United States both from the private and public sectors around the world. Simply put, the numbers show that the more the United States helps the world, the more it helps itself.

Trump says cutting diplomatic outreach and reducing foreign aid commitments are about putting America first, but this is a narrative fallacy because he plans to slash government aid to those who are most in need in his own country. Trump and his administration want to severely curtail social safety nets such as food stamps, supplemental income, rent assistance, education grants, and government-run healthcare programs used by the poor and their children as well as the elderly and disabled. Consider that two-thirds of minimum-wage workers in the United States are women, many of whom have children and are also primary caretakers. Without a social safety net, how can these women and their children break the cycle of poverty?

It would come as a surprise to many of the developing nations of the earth that there are actually poor people in the United States. Of course, there is not the same threat of widespread famine, but there is real poverty that needs to be addressed—poverty caused by racial and gender inequality, lack of educational opportunities, and crushing healthcare bills. Social safety net programs are vital to a thriving society and a functioning democracy, yet time and time again safety net programs are a matter of heated debates between the two major political parties in the United States.

The root of these debates is complex, but there seem to be two major ideologies constantly at war in general politics and even within the human psyche: personal responsibility and shared responsibility. Those who believe primarily in personal responsibility argue that all people have their own bootstraps and they should use those bootstraps to pull themselves up. Each person is responsible only for himself or herself and family. If you're poor, homeless, and/or hungry—get a better-paying job. Those who are well off should not have to pay for those who aren't, and ill health is often the result of bad choices. Personal responsibility might also dictate that it is better for tax cuts to go to those who create jobs, and then somehow the wealth will eventually trickle down to those who are poor and need work.

The shared-responsibility side accepts that poverty is a societal construct, that ill health is often a matter of genes and not choice, and that the rich should pay more to help those who are in the middle and lower classes get a leg up on the social ladder.

These two schools of thought are distinct, but they do sometimes overlap. For example, everyone agrees that taxes are important, as they pay for infrastructure, national defense, the judicial system, oversight agencies that ensure the safety of food, drugs, environment, and so on. You can occasionally get these ideologies to agree on a social safety net such as taxpayer-funded social security or Medicare but, in general, the ideological divide is sharp and clear when it comes to who should have access to social welfare programs.

The personal-responsibility ideologues believe that too much of a safety net is a disincentive to hard work. They believe there is a significant population who will just live off safety nets they have never contributed to (including "illegals" who come to the United States expecting free stuff, despite the fact that immigrants are not eligible for benefits for five years after arrival, and undocumented people contribute to social welfare programs but are not eligible for any). The shared-responsibility ideologues know that at their core, most human beings actually feel shame about their poverty, desperately want to make a better life for themselves and their children, and just need some help along the way. Sure, there are individuals who take advantage of the welfare system, but their numbers are negligible in the grand scheme of things—consider the white-collar crimes of bankers and hedge fund managers that have resulted in millions and even billions of dollars of theft.

Interestingly, both sides of this ideological divide are more than happy to justify their beliefs with the same religious principles: "For each will have to bear his own load" or "Carry each other's burdens." Nowhere is this ideological war being played out more fiercely than in the current battle over healthcare in the United States.

It is incomprehensible to me that the United States is the only developed nation on this earth that does not have universal healthcare. The fact that it is also the wealthiest nation not to have coverage for all people is even more mind- boggling. Mexico, despite still being an emerging economy, today has universal healthcare. I threw myself into the healthcare debate in my own country once I had the legislative power to do so, because I knew from personal experience the life-altering effect of physical ailments. I spent my childhood and early adulthood toiling on my family's farm. Soon after college, I delivered heavy cases of Coca-Cola all around the country. After I quit my corporate job, I went back home and spent years working on the land before I got into political activism. The years of backbreaking work took their toll on my body, and I suffered from spinal problems that eventually required surgery. The pain was often excruciating, but I had access to the best doctors because I had great health insurance and the means to pay for anything else needed. What must it be like for those laborers who toil under the hot sun on both Mexican and U.S. farms without access to doctors? What must it be like for women who have to give birth at home without the benefit of pain medicines? For those who suffer through painful illnesses without any hope for a cure or comfort? The idea of preventable suffering was intolerable to me, and I needed to help do something about it.

As a top-tier employee of Coca-Cola in Mexico, I enjoyed a level of care that only a fraction of Mexicans did. People who have worked for a global corporation know what I mean. But global corporations don't offer this level of care because they believe it is their moral obligation to do so. Their human resources executives don't stay up at night trying to figure out which is the best health insurance provider for their employees out of some deep-seated feeling of compassion and ethical obligation for the shared humanity of their employees. They also don't decide to not offer health insurance because their employees should just feel lucky to have a well-paying job and use their salary to pay doctors directly. The truth is that global corporations have excellent health insurance plans because they have accepted as fact the empirical research that shows employees who have regular access to doctors and are freed from the burdens of fear about unplanned illness make the most productive workers.

I believe that we should take those empirical findings and apply them to the debate about social safety nets in society overall. When people don't have to be afraid of hunger or homelessness or untreated illness, it frees them to be more productive members of society and helps inspire innovation, all of which boosts growth and wages for everyone. In other words, yes, we are each responsible for our own actions, but we all need help and we must always act for one another.

I don't believe any human being should die or enter into bankruptcy because he or she has lost a job or cannot afford medical treatment. It's hard to make sense of people living in the richest country on earth needing to work two full-time jobs to pay basic bills and put food on their table. No young adult should have to forgo an education because of having to work to care for a sick family member. Before I became president of Mexico, only about half of the country had access to healthcare through an employer. The rest of the population paid for healthcare out of pocket, and those who couldn't afford a doctor suffered terribly.

In Mexico, before the advent of true democracy, it was customary for presidents to completely undo the programs that the previous president had created and start all over again. That was not my plan. My administration improved upon things that were working and introduced new legislation where needed, but always kept the focus on what would help the most people. We knew that over half of the population in Mexico did not have any form of health insurance, so we created a healthcare policy called Seguro Popular, or Popular Insurance, which helped pave the way for today's universal health coverage in Mexico.

The initial program did not go as far as I wanted it to, because there were plenty of congressional opponents, remnants of the old dictatorial PRI political party. These political colleagues were still invested in the status quo, which represented powerful special interests. My presidential term ended in 2006, but by the end of President Felipe Calderon's term in 2012, Mexico had official universal coverage. Today, every Mexican citizen has the care, medicines, and whatever lifesaving surgeries they need. There are still parts of the country where there could be more health centers, but no Mexican citizen has to worry about not being able to afford to visit a doctor. Mexico's journey toward healthcare for all is very much like President Barack Obama's journey with the U.S.'s Patient Protection and Affordable Care Act. President Obama went as far as he could given his circumstances, which included unprecedented obstructions from political opponents.

Mexico achieved what the United States is still mired in conflict about by adopting what many would consider a revolutionary approach to healthcare—top down, instead of bottom up. In our program, the young pay for the old, the healthy help pay for the sick, and the rich pay more than the poor. The working theory is that every young person will get old, the healthy may one day get sick, and the rich can afford it. Like the U.S., we have a combination of employer-sponsored, private, and government-run health insurance programs, but every single person, regardless of employment status or income level, is covered. We commissioned studies, we ran algorithms with a multitude of scenarios, and we found that the top-down approach is what worked. Before Obamacare, the United States had it backward—the system was set up so that the sick had to pay more than the healthy, the old more than the young, and the rich weren't tasked with paying more in taxes in order to help the poor afford the already significant premiums. Mexico's system isn't perfect but, like most other developed nations on earth, no one is going to go bankrupt because he or she can't afford basic healthcare.

The healthcare industry represents one-sixth of the United States economy. It is a giant, snarling mess of a business, and it will take time to sort it out, but the way to frame any argument is to always think of the people first. I am no expert in U.S. healthcare policy, but Trump and his cabinet should listen to care providers and patients. Why do health insurance CEOs, administrators, and brokers make hundreds of times more than the doctors, nurses, and home health aides who provide the care? Shouldn't the government be spending more funds on the kinds of medical science and technologies that can help prevent and cure illnesses? How is it possible that people get kicked off their insurance plans because they got sick? How could those with pre-existing conditions not be able to get health insurance? Before the Affordable Care Act, why did women, who are tasked by nature to give birth, have to pay more for bringing life into this world?

These and other issues were directly dealt with in President Obama's signature healthcare legislation. When President Calderon took over after my term was over, he did not rip up Seguro Popular and start over—he improved upon what my administration created so that the system would cover even more people more efficiently. By contrast, instead of keeping what works from President Obama's signature healthcare legislation, and improving on that which needs to be fixed, Trump and his supporters speak only of repealing and replacing. Their obsession feels like a personal vendetta born out of disdain and jealousy of the country's first African American president. Their replacement plans don't sound like plans at all, just steps back to the way things were. They should be working hard to make sure that the most comprehensive system is put in place for the benefit of all.

Despite the constant calls for "America first," it is not the citizens of the United States who are at the forefront of Trump's healthcare agenda; it is clearly the rich, the pharmaceutical companies, the insurance providers, and the special interests. The personal-responsibility ideologues are adamant that the gains that have been made with Obamacare be stripped away from those who need it most by removing protections for pre-existing conditions and gender-equitable costs, and cutting any social programs that subsidize the needs of women, the poor, the elderly and disabled, and children.

Donald Trump continues to say the ACA is failing, that it is already dead, in an effort to stop the momentum of those who oppose his plans. He's lying. The insurance markets are stabilizing, and the ACA's changes to the healthcare industry have saved millions of lives. It is heartening to see the public outcry, the protests, and the people taking to the streets and confronting their legislative representatives. Trump wants to tear the ACA down just for the sake of placing his mark in the history books. His obsessive need for a "win" will backfire on him and his supporters "bigly."

Despite his overtures to the "forgotten men and women," Trump doesn't seem to understand or believe that the needs of the people have to come before the needs of the powerful few. I found it reprehensible when he brazenly told supporters during a rally in Iowa that he would not hire "a poor person" to work in his cabinet because only the rich know how to do the job. I don't remember Trump's making speeches that featured real plans on how to help those who are disadvantaged—there was nothing substantial about the poor, elderly, sick, or disabled. All I remember is his screeches about "winners" and "losers."

The thing is, in Trump's worldview, those who are not like him, the vast majority of the people, are already "losers." To all those who believe the richest country on earth should provide healthcare for all and are right now making calls and fighting to stop the repeal of Obamacare, please keep fighting. This is literally a fight for your lives. The repeal-and-replacement bill that was passed by the U.S. Congress and proposed by the Senate is truly an abomination; it is nothing but a tax cut for the rich disguised as a healthcare plan. Trump's calls to just repeal the ACA or let it fail are clear signs that Trump either is mentally incapable of understanding the implications or simply does not care about bringing on a humanitarian disaster in his own country.

The United States has what many consider to be the greatest democracy on earth—a democracy whose foundations lie in the freedom to choose one's path, responsibility for one's own actions and, above all, a sense of shared fate. At both the global and the national levels, democracy exists along the unbreakable link between personal and shared responsibility. The essential truth about a liberal democracy is that people can't make informed choices about their lives or their government if they are, literally, not well in their own minds and bodies. The wellness of the people is essential to a thriving society. When people are in need, when they are hungry and afraid, they are far more susceptible to populist demagogues and chaos.

The challenge for the United States is to find a way back to that spirit of compassion and collaboration that existed when the Marshall Plan was put in place. The country has made mistakes before, including mistakes made since WW II, but it must heal the fractures exposed by Donald Trump and once again take up the mantle of world leader. I have no doubt that once it does, we can continue working together to heal the global divide that threatens the cherished values of peaceful liberal democracy. As the long-spoon allegory tells us, in a world faced with increasing challenges and boundless potential, either we are going to learn to eat together or we're going to starve alone.

CHAPTER 6

Women and Education

"Human rights are women's rights, and women's rights are human rights."

—HILLARY CLINTON

IN 2012, THE TALIBAN, a group of men who pervert the religion of Islam, ordered the shooting of a young girl named Malala Yousafzai on her way to school. They'd taken over her village in Pakistan and decreed that girls were no longer allowed to go to school. Yousafzai survived a bullet to the head and has gone on to become a symbol of freedom and courage the world over, a winner of the Nobel Prize, and a tireless advocate for the right of women and children to have equal access to education.

Here is what we know about tyrants and authoritarian regimes throughout history: they know women are agents of change, the backbone of the family and community structure. Tyrants also know that to be educated is to be free; people who are able to think critically know how things should and can be and are less susceptible to indoctrination. Those who abuse power do it by systematically denying children education and oppressing women, who literally bring new life into the world. Therefore, we know that two of the overarching challenges we face on our way to a better world, both as individuals and as nations, are gender equity and equal access to education for all.

When I was a child, there were no colleges or universities in my home state. Only the families who were well off could afford to send their children to secondary school, and only the wealthiest could afford to send them to a university. When I was around ten years old, I realized I had a very different life than my friends, the sons and daughters of the families who were employed on our ranch. Instead of going to school and then spending the afternoon playing, these children had to work. By the time I was sent to a Catholic high school in Wisconsin, many of those friends had decided to cross the border in the hope of making enough money to help support their parents and siblings.

I realized then how the cycle of poverty worked. Those who were born poor, those who could not afford to get a higher education, would be poor for life. This realization felt like a shock to my system. For girls in my community, it was even worse. Many girls would not even get a primary education, because their life was relegated to the upkeep of the home. Oftentimes, young girls had to stay home to care for their siblings while their mothers went to work in the fields. The young girls would stay home until they, too, eventually got married and had children of their own. And so the cycle continued...

In fundamentalist authoritarian regimes, women are suffering under regressive policies that forbid their participating in government, working outside of the home, or even traveling without a male guardian; they cannot freely choose who they will marry, and face the death penalty for transgressions such as having a child out of wedlock. Women living in most modern-day democratic societies have more agency over their lives, but there are still millions of women fighting domestic violence and sexual abuse, struggling to gain access to professional development and career growth opportunities along with equal pay and family care policies that would help them stay in the workforce.

There are plenty of developed and developing countries that have elected or have appointed women as heads of state, so I expected the United States, where the women's rights movement has made truly significant gains, to elect Hillary Clinton —by far the most qualified candidate in history—to the office of the presidency. Former first lady, senator, and secretary of state Clinton is a perfect example of a woman from humble beginnings who was able to use the power of her intellect and sheer will to navigate significant obstacles placed on her by society. Hillary Clinton's Ivy League education and professional opportunities could have made her millions in the private sector, but she chose to dedicate her life to the betterment of marginalized people, including poor women and children.

Despite her clear qualifications, Hillary Clinton was a victim of her success. Women often are. Clinton's ambition was seen as insidious and unwomanly. She was criticized for her clothes, hair, and physique, for continuing to work full-time while her husband was a major political figure and for not taking her husband's last name. The savaging of her public image is one of the greatest travesties in the history of American politics. By contrast, Donald Trump's self-professed greed, utter obsession with "getting even," lack of public service, and explicit misogyny were not enough to deter his ascendancy to the presidency.

Hillary Clinton campaigned on a progressive platform that included comprehensive immigration reform, raising the minimum wage, equal pay, women's rights, and making college affordable or debt-free for all. She knows that education is the key to true change. Trump's platform, on the other hand, was insulting to every thinking person—male or female. When a teenaged girl asked Trump during a campaign rally whether he believed women deserved equal pay, he irritatingly responded, "Only if you do as good of a job." Well, the question is, how can a woman do as good a job if society is designed in such a way that women don't have equal individual rights?

Trump, a serial philanderer, has a history of reducing women to sexual objects. His first response on meeting French president Emmanuel Macron's wife on Bastille Day was to gape at her body and say what "good physical shape" she was in and call her "beautiful." Not surprising from a man who owned both the Miss USA and Miss Universe pageants—neither of which I would say exists to showcase women's intellects. Trump has made bizarre comments about his daughter's looks, going so far as to say he would date her if they weren't related. Trump declared that pregnancy is an inconvenience to employers and has said that letting wives work is "very dangerous" because they ignore the home. More than a dozen women have accused him of inappropriate physical contact.

His response to the rise of sexual assaults in the U.S. military was that it is to be expected because men and women now serve together. At his third presidential debate with Hillary Clinton, in addition to hosting the women who'd allegedly had sexual relations with Bill Clinton, Trump quoted a tweet that asked: if Hillary Clinton could not satisfy her husband, how could she satisfy America? Trump cruelly reduced Clinton, by far an intellectually and morally superior political opponent, to nothing but a jilted wife who'd lost her husband's sexual interest.

Trump's insulting and inappropriate comments about women are endless and exhausting, but many hoped he would leave the "boy talk" and "locker room banter" aside when he ascended to the presidency. For men like Trump, power only emboldens. Once Trump became president, he and his administration launched an all-out assault on every significant political gain women have made. He signed executive orders that severely curtailed government aid to health organizations around the world that offered family planning education and disease prevention, and rolled back regulations aimed at equal pay and representation for women.

Using the mantle of "religious freedom," Trump's proposed healthcare plan restricts contraceptive, prenatal, and maternal coverage protections and defunds Planned Parenthood—the leading healthcare provider for disadvantaged women throughout the country. Most recently, Trump's federal budget removed $200 million from an Obama-era teen pregnancy research and prevention program in favor of what appears to be an abstinence-only curriculum—a proven failed policy that leads only to increased teenage pregnancy and abortions. The bottom line is that the Trump administration's goal is to severely curtail women's rights regarding their bodies. It comes as no surprise then, based on what we know about authoritarian governments, that along with repressing women, Trump is assaulting the idea of education itself.

Trump likes to congratulate himself on his own college education and his "good brain" and ability to use the "best words," yet publicly announced that he loved "the poorly educated" and continuously attacks those he considers political, media, and academic "elites." He takes every opportunity to promote anti-intellectual sentiment, which history has shown does not end well. Consider the Khmer Rouge, a xenophobic isolationist regime in Cambodia led by false prophet Pol Pot—its attack on intellectualism is a relatively recent and drastic example of where this can lead. Under the guise of a "people's revolution," Pol Pot and his followers pushed an agenda of national self-sufficiency and anti-elitism that ended in starvation and mass genocide. This did not happen thousands of years ago. This happened in the late 1970s and didn't end until the early '80s. We are talking about just thirty years ago.

Trump's praise of the "poorly educated"—not as a condition to be improved, but as a condition to be proud of—and the way he paints those who are learned as being "out of touch" with society are reckless, especially when—barring a lottery win or inheritance, and even with some kind of highly valued artistic or athletic talent—a higher education is the only way out of poverty. I suspect Trump knows the value of a college education since he, along with all five of his adult children, have one. Trump has gotten to where he is by manipulating and taking advantage of those who don't know better and those who cannot afford lengthy court battles. He knows that a less educated public is more easily duped into believing lies and misleading statements.

I haven't heard Trump promoting educational policies that would truly benefit the people of the United States. Why isn't he talking about strengthening childhood education programs and making higher education affordable for all at a time when millions of jobs are still waiting to be filled because of the large skill and education gaps that prevent workers from applying? What if the United States increased funding for global educational exchange programs, which have been proven to strengthen international relations, foster cultural tolerance, and bring increased investments from abroad into the U.S. economy?

Instead of making it easier for the people of this country to get a fair shot, Trump's federal budget proposes slashing aid to preschool, after-school, and summer-school programs, along with cutting federal grants for college, scholarships for future teachers, and job retraining programs—programs that create and maintain the dynamism and flexibility needed for today's workforce and help disadvantaged families climb the class ladder. We know a proper education is the key to transformative societal change. I firmly believe an entire country could be fundamentally altered in just one generation if every one of its people received a full childhood-to-college education.

The current anti-intellectual sentiment in the United States that propelled Donald Trump to the presidency is surprising in a country that is so well known for innovation. Perhaps this U-turn is rooted in the fact that not only has a higher education become out of reach for so many but that people are turning to warped fundamentalist ideologies. Without an educated citizenry, you are left with ignorance, and ignorance leads to intolerance, fear of change, lack of innovation, and, ultimately, a diminished life expectancy. Every nation should focus on education—a balanced education that includes science, math, computer technology, history, literature, the arts, philosophy, and civic engagement. The wealthiest country in the world should make education available for all. Young adults should not have to forgo a college education simply because their parents can't afford it, or be saddled with loans that lock them into a lifetime of working unfulfilling jobs just to pay them off.

For women, a lack of educational opportunity is especially harsh because they already face political, social, and cultural barriers that prevent them from contributing to and benefitting from society's economic growth. In Mexico, there is a deeply ingrained culture of machismo, of men feeling superior to women. There is a well-known saying in Mexico that women are to be kept like shotguns—loaded and in a corner—something akin to "barefoot and pregnant." And despite all of our advances, much of this type of thinking is still pervasive in Mexican society.

I grew up in a traditional, staunchly Catholic family. My mother, Doña Mercedes, was at stay-at-home mother who seemed to be everywhere at once—working on the farm, tending to the sick and wounded, helping us with our homework, and reinforcing values and ethics-based lessons in our daily lives. I grew up with a deep respect for this incredible woman—to me, she is still larger than life. When I told my family I had decided to go into political activism, my father had already warned us to stay out of politics, and my brothers were fearful of losing our ranch to the PRI dictatorship. They begged me not to do it and said I would ruin the family business and even get myself killed. Only my mother told me to go for it. She said the country couldn't take the tyranny anymore and that it was time for me to help our neighbors. When I eventually ran both for Congress and the governorship, my sister helped organize women's groups that went around the country supporting my candidacy. My mother and sister were integral to the success of my political career and our quest to usher in true democracy in Mexico. I could not have done it without them.

There is another heroic woman without whom I would not be here—my soul mate and wife, la Señora Marta Fox. Marta is my partner and confidante, my equal, if not my superior. Together, Marta and I were determined to address the issues of education and gender inequality in Mexico. As my government was the first truly democratically elected one since the 1920s, my presidency was hailed as a revolution of hope, the dawning of a new era. Marta and I were determined that the revolution of hope would also be a revolution for women and children. Despite the backlash from our traditional society, Marta and I, along with my administration, got to work on a series of programs designed to bring gender equity and educational reform to the newly democratized Mexico.

I have always admired the world-renowned universities in the United States, and while it's true that the U.S. system overall needs improvement, it is a fact that over 80 percent of U.S. children get a high school education and around 70 percent attend college. By contrast, when I came to office in 2000, only 5 percent of our people were able to go to college and many children had an average of just five years of education. I knew there was no way our country could move forward in the globalized economy without a strong educational foundation.

After finally agreeing on a federal budget my first year in office, we created scholarships for millions of poor, rural children so they could stay in school longer instead of having to work or stay home to care for siblings. Our administration also criminalized domestic violence and worked to institute policies that would break the glass ceiling at corporations and advance women's participation in government. We changed the welfare payment structure so that women, instead of male "heads of households," directly received government assistance. We created parenting guides that stressed the importance of parental involvement in schools—which, unlike in the United States, was not common in our country. We empowered the teachers unions, which were made up mostly of women, funded teacher training programs, and increased salaries while also implementing rigorous testing and compliance policies.

Without a doubt, none of the educational reforms could have been achieved without the full support and leadership of the women in the teachers unions. They led the fight for reform, and we are all better off for it. These women even supported the more controversial parts of our plan, which included sex education. I supported the use of the morning-after pill as well as condoms and birth control in our educational outreach. Despite the fact that as a Catholic I am staunchly pro-life, I believe that women should have the right to plan their families and not be exposed to easily preventable sexually transmitted diseases. Research has shown that women who have the ability to plan their families have fewer, healthier children and are in a better position to take advantage of economic and educational opportunities, which fuels GDP growth. Marta dedicated herself to raising private funds for programs that would educate disadvantaged and indigenous women about healthcare issues such as breast and cervical cancer, domestic and substance abuse, sex, maternity, and childbirth safety. My wife helped set up shelters for women and children who had been abused and needed a safe place.

Marta's commitment to uplifting women began early in her life. She was born in the Mexican state of Michoacán to a loving family who encouraged her naturally inquisitive nature. At the age of twelve, she began weekly visits to a women's prison as part of her Catholic school's requirements to help the poor and disadvantaged. The suffering she saw would forever change her, and Marta dedicated the rest of her life to social justice causes and improving the lives of women, children, and the poor.

Even before we met, Marta had run for the mayor of her city (Celaya) in 1993 as part of the same opposition Nation Action Party (PAN) I belonged to. Sadly, her campaign did not win, but we would end up meeting, working together, eventually falling in love, and winning the presidency almost a decade later. Despite all the good Marta had accomplished, overt and implicit misogyny had a negative effect on her career. Much like with Hillary Clinton and other prominent women, my wife's desire to hold a place in government and her public campaign for the rights of women and the poor were tarnished by allegations of corruption and financial misdealing. My wife is beloved by the disadvantaged and the marginalized indigenous communities, and this makes her dangerous to those in power.

Marta became the target of carefully coordinated media efforts by political opponents, who accused her of hiding a future presidential bid of her own, and they tried to convince people that I would rig the system so that she would win. None of it was true. Marta is to this day a tireless advocate for women and children and an incredibly talented fundraiser who continues to draw attention and support to their struggle. She will not be deterred. She will persist.

Along with the brave and unbreakable women in the Mexican teachers unions, the female lawmakers who supported our reforms, my wife, and the women in my family, I count among my heroes women like Mother Teresa, who taught the world about empathy for the poorest among us regardless of their religious faith, and Rosa Parks, who risked her life to help usher in the civil rights movement by refusing to give up her bus seat to a white passenger.

Women are the key to resisting Donald Trump. His administration is taking points straight from the tyrannical playbooks of history. Remember that along with draconian deportation policies, one of the cruel immigration-deterring tactics floated to the media by the Trump administration was to separate women from their children at the border. Any overtures about "women's empowerment" and "respect for women" from Trump's mouth are nothing but lip service and distractions meant to keep the population docile and complicit.

Women's leadership in today's world is essential for humanity's progress. The social ills of intolerance, racism, and class and gender inequality can be remedied only through education, empathy, and civic engagement. We cannot forget that the male youths who shot Malala Yousafzai were themselves victims of their own ignorance, manipulated by men who pervert religion in order to oppress others. Yousafzai survived to remind us all that "one child, one teacher, one book, and one pen can change the world."

Let's get to work.

PART 3

HOPE

Justice and the Truth,
Democracy and True Leaders,
Spirituality and the
Way Forward

CHAPTER 7

Justice and the Truth

"The arc of the moral universe is long, but it bends toward justice."

—Theodore Parker, (later quoted by
Martin Luther King Jr.)

WE ARE ALL FAMILIAR with the image of Lady Justice as a blindfolded woman holding scales in one hand and a sword in the other. Lady Justice has roots both in ancient Egyptian and Greco-Roman cultures. The blindfold represents impartiality; everyone, regardless of background, is supposed to be equal before the law. Justice requires that we tell the truth. The scales measure our words and the intent of our deeds, and the sword represents the harbinger of order. Human beings are fallible; our actions are warped by our biases, and those are defined by what we are taught, but the moral core of justice is always truth. Without truth there is no justice, and without justice there is no peace. Laws were created to keep the balance,

stability, and harmony in society—these are the universal principles that justice attempts to restore if threatened.

Representative democracy, as modeled by the United
States and other nations, though imperfect, has proven to be
the best system of governance in our quest to keep order and
foster prosperity. The people's belief and trust in every lever of
democratic government—legislative, executive, and judicial—
is crucial. A society in which the people don't believe they are
represented, where they have no way to address their grievances,
where their voices are not heard, will never be stable for long.
The Constitution of the United States, emulated by emerging
democracies around the world, stands as one of the greatest
documents of governance ever written, and has allowed for the
peaceful transfer of power in the U.S. for the past two hundred
years—a remarkable feat.

The Constitution's strength lies in the idea that each
branch of government operates independently, and that those
who govern do so by the will of the people. The separation of
powers ensures the checks and balances that prevent a tyrannical
government from controlling the populace, and while the
"majority" rules according to the vote, the rights of individuals
and minority groups are preserved and protected. The free press,
though not a branch of government, is a bulwark of democracy.
The people believe in their government as long as the actions
and motivations of the government are transparent. The rule of
law and the right of the public to be informed are inviolable
principles of true democracies. The judiciary and the free press
are often the first two institutions attacked and then absorbed
by burgeoning authoritarian movements seeking to shut down

democratic governments. In the wrong hands, the judiciary and the free press can be turned from tools of freedom to tools of oppression.

Mexico, with its transition to true democracy in recent years, is presently undergoing a radical transformation of its judicial system. In partnership with the U.S., Mexico's courts now grant open hearings and give more rights to those accused of crimes. Despite the democratic judicial system's greatness, however, it is not without faults. The reality is that laws are not always applied fairly and we must recognize that race, class, and gender directly affect the way we experience justice. Those who are rich have access to the kind of representation that most do not. This is why we often see people of wealth avoid responsibility or punishment for actions that would imprison others.

Donald Trump is one such person. Ironically, a man embroiled in over 3,500 legal actions on everything from financial fraud to educational fraud and sexual improprieties swept into power as the "law and order" candidate. Trump has always used his wealth and influence to circumvent laws—going so far as to brag about paying off politicians in order to get favorable tax breaks for his real estate deals. He is a perfect example of how money can corrupt the system of justice—small-business owners and contractors who could not afford protracted legal battles simply walked away with empty hands after he defrauded them. It's hard to believe a man like this won over sizable portions of the working and middle classes of the population, but Trump used the most historically useful tool of the demagogue—fear. He recast the United States as a dystopian nightmare, a country full of unemployed citizens barely surviving the "carnage" wreaked upon them by undocumented immigrants stealing their jobs and resources, terrorist Muslims, and African American and Latino criminals. In such a chaotic landscape, only a "strong man" can protect you.

To understand the mental gymnastics involved in believing Trump's view of America, one has to know the facts. Violent crime is at a historic low in the country, but America has the highest incarceration rates in the entire world. With less than 5 percent of the world's population, the U.S. imprisons almost 25 percent of it. One out of every five people in jail today is in for a drug offense. The forty-plus years war on drugs has disproportionately affected the poor and minority communities. While there is no substantial difference in the use of drugs between white and minority communities, minorities are up to six times more likely to be imprisoned. The war on drugs has wrecked millions of lives, broken up families, and overburdened federal, state, and local jails, all at taxpayers' expense without any significant lowering of drug use or drug-related crimes. It is not working because the demand for drugs hasn't changed.

The continued criminalization of drugs has served only to empower the black market drug trade and the violence that continues to destabilize nations such as Mexico. Trump's Department of Justice has rewound the clock on President Obama's prison and crime reforms that have done away with draconian prison sentences for nonviolent drug offenders, curtailed the rise of private prisons for profit that incentivize incarceration, and overseen the legalization of drugs like marijuana throughout many states in the country. The imprisonment of nonviolent drug offenders has ruined the future of many youths who are plagued with criminal records that prevent them from getting jobs and access to educational opportunities that would allow them to contribute to society. Seeing no way out, these youths stay on the paths that lead many right back to jail.

This senseless war on drugs has also diverted much-needed resources from education, job training, medical research, and social safety nets that would improve the nation far more than imprisonment. Similar to the United States' war on drugs, Mexico's judicial system and the tragic legacy of the cartels have laid waste to millions of lives without addressing the root causes. Our country has the added burden of rampant corruption— from judges to politicians and enforcement agency officials at every level. We need to address the problem from another angle.

Marijuana has now been legalized in twenty-nine states in the U.S.—by regulating consumption, production, and distribution instead of criminalizing medical and recreational drug use, the states stand to make almost $7 billion in revenue. We should treat drugs the way we treat alcohol and cigarettes. While there is no disagreement that drugs are social ills, the way to deal with them is to educate people about the effects of what they put into their bodies, create laws that dictate use, and then let them make up their own minds. The story of Adam and Eve is about natural human curiosity and free will—they wanted to know what the fruit of forbidden knowledge tasted like. When it comes to drugs, the better way is to not forbid and criminalize, but to inform and regulate.

It is this idea of the law being an instrument of social stability that I continue to think about when I watch Trump speak. I remember being incredulous when Trump said, on live television, that he could literally shoot someone on Fifth Avenue in Manhattan and not lose any supporters. Let's step back for a moment. Many pundits took the statement to be about the kind of blind loyalty of his followers. The truth, however, is even more frightening—what Trump really did was declare himself above the law. He said he could kill someone and not face the judicial consequences of murder. How do we convince desperate youths not to join violent gangs when a world leader can speak like this with impunity?

As president, Trump has gone on to systematically attack the judicial branch of the United States government. Like a third-world dictator, he has repeatedly called for the investigation and jailing of Hillary Clinton, ignorant of or not caring about the fact that his executive powers don't extend to imprisoning political opponents. Trump duped thousands of innocent, hardworking Americans with a real estate course scam called Trump University, and outrageously accused the presiding judge in the fraud case of being unable to render impartial judgment because he was "Mexican." Despite his denials of wrongdoing, Trump settled for $25 million, but his privilege allowed him to do so without admitting fault.

When the Fourth and Ninth Circuit federal courts struck down Trump's Muslim ban, he questioned the legitimacy of the "so-called judge" and said the courts were "too political." He then tweeted to his supporters that they should blame the courts for any future terrorist attacks, leading to many judges' receiving death threats and prompting them to increase their security detail. That the freest country on this earth has a sitting president actively telling people to go after judges is not just concerning, it is downright terrifying. Former acting attorney general Sally Yates, fired for refusing to obey the order for Trump's Muslim ban, recently wrote, "President Trump's actions appear aimed at destroying the fundamental independence of the Justice Department. All the while, he's ripping the blindfold off Lady Justice and attempting to turn the department into a sword to seek vengeance against his perceived enemies and a shield to protect himself and his allies." So far, despite Trump's efforts, the courts have kept him in check and the corresponding bureaucracies of the government have followed the letter of the law.

Trump thinks of himself as a king, surrounded by his heirs; he believes he is still the head of the Trump Organization whose children work with him and not the president of a country. Like a movie mafia don, Trump fired FBI director James Comey after he refused Trump's request for a pledge of absolute loyalty. Thankfully, Comey's written recollection of events, picked up by the press, eventually led to the creation of two separate ongoing investigations in the Senate and congressional legislative bodies and an independent special counsel. In other words, the government of the United States is checking Trump, and despite his best efforts to discredit those who are dissenting, what is clear is that Trump is hiding something, and whatever he is hiding is more important to him than the rule of law.

Laws matter, but it also matters who creates them and the motivations behind how they are interpreted. Laws are societal constructs; what happens when laws are decreed by the likes of men who see themselves as beyond them? There can be no peace with men who believe some people aren't worthy of equal protection under their laws. There can be no peace when a man like Trump calls out for the return of torture and casually speaks of eradicating terrorism by killing the innocent families of terrorists. There will be no stability with mass deportations and divisive rhetoric that leads millions of ethnic minorities to live in fear.

Trump refused to divest his private business. He seems to be clearly profiting from the office of the presidency, prompting the director of the independent Office of Government Ethics to resign and publicly condemn Trump's behavior. Make no mistake, the Constitution of the United States, the rule of law, the very idea of truth as the moral core of justice are all under assault by Trump and his administration, but the people of the United States and her allies should have faith in the Constitution. Trump, safely ensconced within the walls of the White House, is testing the boundaries of the law; he does not feel compelled by propriety or appearances, but it is clear that there is a feature of democracy he both loves and fears more than any other: the free press.

There is a Mexican proverb, *"El pez muere por la boca,"* which translates as "The fish dies by the mouth," because we know that the mouth swallows the hook. Donald Trump will end his own presidency and destroy the credibility of all those who aid and abet him, through his own words. It can be argued that the mainstream journalistic media played a big part in Trump's election by engaging in false equivalencies in the name of fairness and objectivity—meaning it presented Trump and Hillary Clinton as two sides of the same coin, when the truth of the matter is that Trump was an aberration and a threat to the very ideals of the country and should have been treated as such. Some argue that the media is really no more to blame for Trump's election than those who voted for him, but regardless of anyone's view on fault, the media is essential to democracy. The free press keeps the people informed and ensures transparency in the actions of those who govern.

I remember after I won the Mexican presidency how thrilling it was to see the resurgence of the press in a country that had what amounted to state-controlled media for so many years. The thrill was tempered somewhat at times by how surreal it also felt to see cartoons and articles that appeared to completely distort my comments and intentions. I was rarely personally offended, but I was hurt by the treatment of my wife, Marta. Marta eventually sued and won a lawsuit against a publication for outright slander. However, both of us and my administration knew that the resurgence of the free press was also an indicator that our emerging democracy was real, and no one ever thought anything should be done legislatively to curtail its freedom. We know that lies, gossip, rumors, and bad actors can make the truth hard to find in today's media, but under no circumstances should the press ever be controlled or censored by the government. Rather, we should concentrate on creating an educated electorate who can think critically and can tell the difference between truth meant to inform and fiction meant to entertain.

History has shown us the power of state-run media to sanction human rights catastrophes like in those in North Korea, Nazi Germany, and the Rwandan genocide. Still, even in the United States, a country whose people enjoy a high degree of personal and intellectual freedom, the media can still be manipulated into obfuscating and providing a false narrative.

It is a fact that a combination of doctored intelligence reports, innuendo, and outright lies fueled by fears after the 9/11 terrorist attack led the United States into war with Iraq. President George W. Bush's legacy will forever be marred by the deaths of hundreds of thousands of Iraqi civilians and thousands of U.S. soldiers based on the lie that Saddam Hussein had weapons of mass destruction. Let me be clear, President Bush is a principled man whom I respect to this day and with whom I share many personal and political views. President Bush and I developed a deep trust in the years before we both became presidents, but despite our closeness, I could not support the war in Iraq.

For the better part of a year, President Bush tried to convince me that Saddam Hussein was a tyrant hell-bent on destroying his people and that he supported terrorist organizations. President Bush would eventually send Colin Powell and Condoleeza Rice to Mexico several times with charts and fuzzy aerial photographs of compounds that they insisted held weapons of mass destruction. To us, the data seemed surprisingly thin, especially from a country with the most advanced intelligence technology available. It's difficult for some to hear this, but I know that President Bush's intentions came from what he felt was a moral imperative in addition to a political one—he wanted the eradication of future terrorist threats and the preservation of burgeoning democratic movements in the Middle East.

Besides the fact that President Bush was getting faulty advice from his aides, he was blinded to the core truth of democracy. I believe that Saddam was a dictator who was oppressing his people and killing innocents, but I also know that you cannot topple a dictator with violence and hope to bring about democracy with outside brute force, rumors, hypocrisy, or lies. Democracy can truly be ushered in only by the will of the country's people, and when true democracy is accepted, it settles over the people in a nonviolent manner. Neither I nor any Mexican government officials ever felt there was credible proof that Saddam had WMDs. We practically begged President Bush to bring the matter of war to the deliberative body of the United Nations Security Council and then wait for the findings of UN weapons inspectors before making any decisions.

Despite the pressure from top- and midlevel U.S. diplomats and even suggestions that immigration reform could be returned to the forefront of the national conversation should we support the war, Mexico did not waver. We simply could not just invade a sovereign nation without more discussion about the implications of war and procedural plans for a postliberated Iraq. As a country that has been invaded so many times, Mexico knows the cost of war, the suffering of families who lose their loved ones, the deaths of young adults who do not live long enough to have families of their own.

Despite the ongoing discussions at the UN, it was clear Bush had already made up his mind. He withdrew his resolution from the Security Council and invaded Iraq. Even though Mexico did not go to war as a country, we still went to war as a people. Mexican nationals living in the U.S. promised fast-tracked citizenships joined the military, and already enlisted Mexican Americans headed to Iraq. It is a little known fact that Mexicans total over 55 percent of all Latinos in the United States army. My refusal to join the coalition of the willing distanced President Bush and myself, and practically froze all talks of immigration reform and guest-worker programs, although our friendship remained strong throughout the rest of our presidencies. History has proved that Mexico made the right decision, even if it cost us significant political and diplomatic capital with the U.S. There were massive antiwar protests in the U.S. and around the world, but the government's tunnel vision on WMDs and the media's complicity in the lead-up to the Iraq War allowed the majority of the people to believe the government's claims.

The same tunnel vision and fatalistic view of the future that led to the Iraq War also gave us Donald Trump. As I said, President Bush was a man of principle, a patriot who truly did care about the people of his country. Trump, despite belonging to the same political party, is no such man. He lives in a prison of his own delusions. What to make of a man who believes and spreads conspiracy theories and refuses to accept facts? Trump's earliest and perhaps most notorious conspiracy theory, which he eventually had to disavow, was that President Barack Obama was a Kenyan-born Muslim. Of course, Trump's proof was an "incredibly credible source," and the purpose was nothing more than an effort to delegitimize the nation's first African American president.

Trump's claim that he would've won the popular vote had it not been for three to five million illegal voters was based on many friends' telling him that people were at the polls who did not look like they should be voting. His obsession with losing the popular vote led to his commissioning a voter fraud panel that is really an abuse of taxpayer dollars based on a fantasy.

Like his attacks on the integrity of the judiciary, Trump's attack on the media with his #FakeNews campaign is an attempt to discredit journalists and the very idea of an objective truth.

Trump is right that there is a rise of fake online news sites and click-bait headlines that deliberately attempt to fool people. However, he is not discrediting ridiculous Facebook posts; he is going after respected institutions like *The New York Times* and *The Washington Post* and serious television networks like CNN and MSNBC. Trump is both taking advantage of and amplifying a powerful anti-intellectual post-truth movement. One Trump supporter believed a conspiracy theory that began on the internet about Hillary Clinton's running a pedophile ring out of a pizza shop in Washington D.C., and he showed up with a rifle. How different are Trump's shrieks of "fake news" from Hitler's fervent cries of "*Lügenpresse*" (lying press)?

Much like Trump, Hitler's argument was that the media was opposed to his campaign of national and economic independence for Germany. Trump's argument is almost exactly the same—he is here to put "America first" and protect Western ideals from foreigners, but the fake news just keeps standing in his way. Not a single week has gone by in Trump's presidency when he hasn't complained about the media. Trump's treatment of journalists who do not give him "fair" (read: positive) coverage is brutal and downright insulting, and he has threatened to shut down press briefings altogether.

Journalists are risking their lives all around the world to bring us the truth. In Mexico, so many have lost their lives or have disappeared by exposing the cartels and the corruption that continues to blight our government and every level of our judicial system. Journalists deal with so many dangers in their pursuit of the truth to keep the public informed. They shouldn't be taunted, degraded, and undermined by their own government's leaders. It is true that there is a tendency in some of the media to report more about what is wrong with society than what is great, and this creates a sense of constant danger and exaggerated threats. Some would criticize that the mainstream media is more interested in ratings than truth, but the other side of that coin is that it is only feeding our natural appetite for sensationalism.

Trump took advantage of this need for sensationalism with his reimagining of America as a decaying landscape, overrun by brown and black criminals. This is what every single demagogue does—creates the nightmare and then feeds the people the monsters to blame. Trump makes up facts, and when those facts are exposed as lies, he makes up several more and denies he ever said the first one. He is tortured by imagined conspiracy theories that keep him up into the early morning and that he spreads via Twitter to his willing and slavish base of supporters. He is a profoundly ignorant man—ignorant of history, devoid of any appreciation for culture outside of his own, lacking in grace and compassion and, worst of all, he is surrounded by ill-chosen opportunistic advisors.

The truth means nothing to Trump, who has no issue taking credit for others' work, inventing people who don't exist, or recounting things that never happened, like his viciously bigoted lie that he personally saw thousands of Muslims cheering the fall of the Twin Towers. Trump has claimed he lost hundreds of friends at the World Trade Center, yet there is no record of his attending a single funeral or donating to a 9/11-related charity. What is the inner world of a man who can falsely claim friendship with hundreds of people who perished in one of the most horrific ways imaginable, and do it for political points? What kind of person can slander an entire culture to sow division and hatred? *The New York Times* has reported that Trump has intentionally lied almost every day of his presidency. There is simply no politician, much less one who has ascended to the office of the presidency, in the observable history of the country who has behaved this way.

Donald Trump's assault on the truth has eroded the foundation of political discourse to the point where he can tweet that "the press is the enemy of the American people," and before we can even put together cogent arguments about the unconstitutionality of this statement, he is personally attacking a Republican senator and making demonstrably false statements about governmental policy. With all the fear and anxiety that Trump's election has caused, take refuge in the fact that so many people are talking about the concepts of truth and justice and the rule of law in ways they weren't before. Journalism and the media have seen a renewed vigor and renewed interest. People are waking up because they can sense the danger Trump represents. Newspaper and journal subscriptions have increased. The people are becoming more engaged.

Democracy is not something our leaders do while we go about the business of our day. Democracy is something that we must all pay attention to, constantly be vigilant of, and participate in. Martin Luther King Jr. told us (quoting Theodore Parker), "The arc of the moral universe is long, but it always bends toward justice." It bends because the people rise and speak truth to power. We can place our hopes in the rule of law and the free press in both the United States and her democratic allies around the world, who are daily uncovering and exposing Trump's lies and half-truths. Until then, we should all go about the business of gathering our strength and heeding the words of the great writer William Faulkner, "Never be afraid to raise your voice for honesty and truth and compassion against injustice and lying and greed."

CHAPTER 8

Democracy
and True Leaders

*"The people of these United States are the rightful masters
of both congresses and courts, not to over-throw the
Constitution, but to overthrow the men who pervert the
Constitution."*

—Abraiiam Lincoln

Donald Trump's ascendancy to power reminds me of
the rise of populist demagogues in Latin America's fragile
democracies. A charismatic leader would pander to the nation's
poorest and least educated, blame foreign imperialists for the
perils of the economy, scream about love of country, and promise
to fix everything in no time at all. Soon after being elected, the
leader would yell that the nation's continuing economic erosion
was because the government's institutions were run by corrupt
elites and were restraining him or her from making true change.
The leader would call for adjustments or the complete eradication

of a few bureaucracies so the promises to the people could be kept. Soon after this, the courts would start to be packed with those sympathetic to the leader's ideology, the military would be incentivized, and then the threats and jailing and torture of civilian dissenters, journalists, and opposition leaders would begin. An apathetic public, intent on surviving, goes about its days, while those who see what is coming continue to take to the streets yelling for others to wake up, and some are even willing to die for freedom. Meanwhile, the leader amasses more power, continues to make disastrous economic policies both in the private and public sectors that seem to benefit only them and loyalists, hands out symbolic trinkets to the poor, and commissions infrastructure projects such as housing and parks, all in the name of "the people."

This is what is happening right now in Venezuela. Populist Hugo Chavez came to power in 1999 and with him disastrous nativist fiscal policies, centralization of power, and human rights abuses that have sent Venezuela into a tailspin. After Chavez's death, his successor, President Nicolás Maduro, removed the mask from the "benevolent socialism" that Chavez was mostly able to maintain with the country's vast oil profits. But with falling oil prices and overall bad economic policies, what began as a socialist revolution in a democratic and prosperous country is today swiftly turning into a full dictatorship.

Venezuelan society is in an absolute decline, with shortages of basic goods such as toilet paper and medicines. Food insecurity is high, many of the people cannot find enough to eat, and violence has exploded as protestors clash with the Maduro-loyal military and armed pro-government civilian groups. Maduro's response is to point the finger at everything from corrupt elites to the imperialist United States and other dark international forces. The opposition leaders and civilians called for Maduro's removal and, predictably, the leader announced a state of emergency that gave the state power over the distribution of goods, and then called for sweeping changes to the foundations of the country's democratic institutions so he can more efficiently bring relief directly to the people. It's the same old story. We lived with it in Mexico for over seventy years.

I am no longer president of Mexico, but I have dedicated the rest of my life to working for social justice and democracy and to opposing the hypocrisy and fraudulence of populist demagogues and authoritarian states—whether benevolent-seeming ones like the PRI-led government in Mexico that showed a good face to the world while killing, imprisoning, and disenfranchising people behind a curtain, or the more overt ones that behead their people in public. It is because of this commitment to democracy and to freedom that I visited Venezuela along with other heads of state on July 17, 2017, to show our solidarity and our support for those who oppose Maduro's naked grab for more power.

Most recently, Maduro announced that the only way to stop the violence and get the people back to work and eating again was to rewrite the constitution. The constitution would be rewritten by a constituent assembly chosen by "the people" (of course, the majority of those candidates are already loyal to the leader). Most people can see what Maduro is doing—making a sweeping attempt to do away with opposition forces in the legislative body and, if all goes the right way, even enacting a statute that would make Maduro head of state for the rest of his natural life.

A symbolic plebiscite on July 17 was called to count all those who opposed the constitutional initiative ahead of the government-sanctioned vote on July 30. The purpose was to prove his actions were against the will of the people. I accepted the invitation to oversee the voting process along with other political thought leaders, which included the former presidents of Bolivia, Colombia, and Costa Rica. Our goal was to show solidarity with those suffering under Maduro's regime and to show them they were not alone. The entire world is watching despite Maduro's attempt to wall off the country by censoring the free press and shutting down the people's access to foreign media outlets like CNN. Because the majority of the citizenship has access to smartphones and can communicate freely and coordinate protests through them, Maduro has also moved to restrict the internet. Still, it was incredible to see how the populace was able to get around these blocks and continue to mobilize. We spoke with the parents of murdered and imprisoned protestors both civilian and military, the artists whose voices are being silenced, and the students who are being beaten in the streets.

Even with Maduro's increasingly brutal repression, roughly one-quarter of Venezuela's population, over seven million people, came out and voted against Maduro—intellectuals, small-business owners, students, doctors, nurses, service members, the elderly, people from every single place in society risked their lives to make their voices heard. They are calling for a military that respects the law and protects all of the people. They are calling for the rule of law that is supposed to treat everyone equally—regardless of whether in a majority or minority party. In short, the Venezuelan people are calling for democracy and real solutions to the economic crisis.

To the surprise of no one who has lived under or studied the populist playbook, the Venezuelan authorities then accused me of promoting violence and being part of an international conspiracy to intervene in a sovereign nation, and publicly announced I was banned for life from ever visiting the country. On July 30, 2017, Maduro held his vote, inflated his numbers, and ushered in the end of Venezuela's democracy. Like Trump, who installed his daughter and son-in-law in the White House, both Maduro's wife and son were "voted" into the National Assembly.

The only way to bring down the false prophets is to speak directly to their sense of power with the conviction of truth, to shine a light on every single dereliction of duty and abuse. This is what I had to learn to do when I became a political activist and later ran for government. In 1987, I joined the opposition National Action Party (PAN) and the following year announced a run for Congress. The government responded by finding sanitation issues in our state-of-the-art frozen-vegetable plant and shutting it down. Then it revoked our business permits, and our agricultural loans were recalled at the bank so that we would be unable to buy seed. We also employed hundreds of workers at our cowboy boot plant, and the PRI-controlled labor unions told the workers to strike. The PRI was putting us out of business.

I was scared and my brothers were furious, but with the support of my mother and my mentor, farmer and political activist Manuel Clouthier, I was encouraged to keep going, to get louder, to hit back with my voice—to publicly denounce and expose them all. If you are going down, go down fighting. Those in power count on the people's silence. There had been rumblings of change in Mexico, and the people had elected members of the opposition parties to Congress, including myself. The people were starting to get tired of the PRI, but the PRI kept winning the majority with fraudulent elections that gave them the veneer of public support. As the economy continued to decline, protests, mass rallies, and hunger strikes erupted around the country.

Later that year, during municipal elections, I joined fellow dissenters to prove the executive branch was stuffing ballot boxes. We showed up at a polling place in a rural area and attempted to take a few boxes with us. For our troubles, a PRI loyalist stuck a pistol in my belly. I stood down and we went home. I certainly did not want to die, and we already had plenty of faked ballots, which we prominently displayed on whatever state-controlled media would grant us a few minutes of airtime. That same year, the opposition party lost the presidency by a razor-thin margin after the lights went out in the federal election's headquarters and the voting machines mysteriously failed.

I and opposition colleagues continued our civil disobedience, and this time headed to the federal election tribunal and demanded to be allowed to see the ballot boxes held behind a locked door. We linked arms and faced down the military this time. Unlike PRI loyalists with their guns, the army men had rifles with bayonets pointed straight at us. We demanded they let us pass in the name of the Mexican people. Instead, the soldiers cocked their rifles, and we heard the words no one ever wants to hear: "Ready! Aim!…" At that point, we had a choice. As the civil disobedience heroes we had studied—Mahatma Gandhi, Martin Luther King, Václav Havel, and Nelson Mandela—had showed us, we chose to live. But the die was cast for the PRI dictatorship, and the fires of freedom had already been set in the hearts of the people. They knew the truth. The PRI dictatorship would crumble only twelve years later, and I would be elected president.

Democracy is only as strong as the will of the people. Know that those who seek to oppress do so by attacking the people's trust in the institutions of democracy. The oppressors strip people of their vote, strip them of their voice by removing the right to protest and dissent, and strip them of true representation in government, all while wrapping themselves up in the country's flag. I have been outspoken about the need for open markets and liberal democracy, and have consistently condemned the human rights abuses, corruption, and state-controlled cronyism of populist demagogues around the world who use their country's wealth to reward loyalists and punish opponents. This led to severe confrontations during my presidential administration. Hugo Chavez called me "Bush's lapdog" and physically threatened me, Fidel Castro blasted me for taking a stand at the UN against his oppressive policies, and I sustained deep political wounds from Mexico's own eternal presidential candidate/ demagogue in the making, Andrés Manuel López Obrador, who fired up thousands of citizens with conspiracy theories about my close relationship with the United States.

Despite all of the criticism I have taken, from heads of states to everyday Mexican civilians, I continue to believe that the free market and democratic institutions are the best way for countries to prosper and maintain peace. Even with Donald Trump's election, my unshakable belief in the ideals of the United States has not wavered, although I am worried. Those who believe that the country is too big and that her institutions are too strong to go the way of Venezuela are mistaken. It can happen, but we must not let it.

While some may accuse me of romanticizing the ideals and the promise of democracy as written in the U.S. Constitution, this does not mean that I don't recognize America's bloody history—the plight of Native Americans, the enslavement of African Americans, Japanese internment camps, nativist immigrant exclusion acts, domestic and international wars, and regime changes—but all nations need not look far back in their histories to see the worst of human nature. And yet, the United States remains the shining city on the hill, the beacon of hope for freedom around the entire world, and those who seek to dim that light will not succeed as long as the people believe in its promise and work hard to maintain it.

America's racist history is a real and painful wound, but it is also true that out of those wounds America has shown the world that a multiethnic, fully democratic country can achieve peace—a peace that has lasted for almost three centuries no less. The promise the United States makes to its people is the freedom to be and to become, and it is the responsibility of every generation to leave a version of a more perfect union for the next.

The United States is a nation of laws, a nation founded on equality and personal liberty, a nation that has helped liberate more people from tyranny and lifted more people out of poverty than any other. This country requires people of integrity, competence, compassion, and extreme stability to lead it. Donald Trump, whose personality is steeped in narcissism and driven by pure ego, who believes in the racist theory of genetics as opposed to excelling through dedication and experience, is a man who will steer us straight into catastrophe. We can see this already with his garish diplomacy-by-tweets that has destabilized foreign relations with Asia, Latin America, Europe, and the Middle East. Trump's bizarre rants and complete ignorance of foreign and domestic policy, not to mention lack of basic social graces, lead me to think he could not pass a mental hygiene test.

I have said that democracy is only as strong as the will of the people, and it is also true that the will of the people is expressed through the leaders they choose. Now, putting aside the question of whether Trump was actually legitimately chosen, given his loss of the popular vote, the fact is that he does not have the qualifications to lead any democratic nation because he lacks the ability to self-reflect and course-correct. His inability to see his own flaws is a major problem. He cannot swallow his oversized sense of pride; he cannot admit defeat, ask for forgiveness, or seem like he is retreating from a position. He is not flexible or open to new ideas. Trump's mind is fossilized or necrotized, stuck on a view of the world that does not allow for either compromise or growth. There are no colors in his black-and-white world. Trump is incapable of self-reflection.

The Trump leadership is more suited to an authoritarian state than it is to a multiethnic, geographically diverse country. This means that the guardrails of the judicial and legislative bodies, along with the free press and the full participation of the people, are more important today than they ever have been.

Like Donald Trump, both my educational and professional backgrounds are in business. Unlike Trump, who managed to sell people on the myth that his success in business would make him a great president, I know that democratic government is incompatible with traditional corporate-style management. The two ideological ends of the leadership spectrum are the authoritative and the inclusive. In the corporate world, the authoritarian rules—it's top-down delegation. In the corporate world, the power is concentrated at the top and orders are issued down, and followed under penalty of firing. There is little to no room for negotiation, and loyalty is based more on fear of loss than respect. The inclusive style of the leadership spectrum earns the loyalty and respect of the people. There is always room for negotiation. The carrot is more important than the stick. Leaders in the inclusive style know that what you can accomplish through love, not fear, lasts much longer than what you can accomplish through fear.

This is why a truly democratic government cannot simply be installed by waging a war and unseating a dictator—the people have not yet learned what it is to be free and will just seek another authoritarian leader. The people won't truly believe in a free democracy unless they know what it is and yearn for it. This is why the Arab Spring, though looked upon with such hope by many of us, didn't democratize the Arab world in the way we understand democracy. It is true that false prophets can achieve change in their nation really quickly with corporate management, because people fear power and loss, but what is achieved will not last and eventually the people will revolt.

Trump's instincts are Machiavellian; his deal-making is based on a series of threats and a show of force at all times meant to humiliate people into complying. He is not a man to be trusted with the world's most powerful military and nuclear arsenal. I do not believe that a country whose very foundation is freedom will take his orders for long. A true leader must balance strength of character with compassion, must allow intellectual curiosity to be guided by the lessons of history, and must have emotions weighted by reason and facts. Leaders must appreciate diversity in cultures and ideas, and must respect the importance of art to human development. They should be guided by a sense of responsibility for others and have a willingness to listen and negotiate, not demand. They don't see those who opposed their candidacy as enemies or "haters" but as people whom they must find common ground with.

The key to a sustained democracy is to have an educated populace that actively seeks leaders that represent these ideals and to have a consistently engaged public that holds its leaders accountable. Thomas Jefferson, one of the founding fathers of the United States, said that when people fear their government, there is tyranny, but when the government fears its people, there is liberty. Trump doesn't seem to understand that he works for all of the people, not just the ones who elected him.

Donald Trump's election feels illegitimate because he violated the spirit of the country in which he rose to power. It is baffling to me that the powers that be in the United States allowed a man to run for president who refused to show his tax returns after promising to show them over and over again. Now Trump, borrowing heavily from the populist playbook, is calling for the jailing of his political opponents and the censoring of journalists and government whistle-blowers, is calling into question the legitimacy of judges, is undermining the integrity of the voting system by saying three to five million people voted illegally, and is delegitimizing dissenting voices by spreading the conspiracy theory that protestors are paid by his political opponents. He has systematically attacked every foundation of democracy. Only the cognitive dissonance of Trump's base allows them to ignore his fraudulence.

I said earlier that there is a point in the authoritarian government where the people refuse to believe the lies they are told. This is true. Trump said that not even his killing someone in cold blood would turn away his loyalists, the "forgotten people" he says he is serving. He's wrong. Let me be clear that I harbor no illusions that those within his base who feel free to unleash their racism and bigotry can be convinced in the immediate future with appeals to their conscience and moral arguments about our shared humanity. But there are many more people in that base who are looking for the jobs that Trump promised them and are turning a blind eye to his hatred of immigrants and marginalized groups. Trump wrote a big check that at some point he's going to have to cash. He promised a wall, mass deportations, and jobs. People who bought into his myths need tangible evidence of his promises, and they will eventually realize that Trump never pays his bills. Not even Trump's blue-collar-billionaire appeal will save him then.

Donald Trump is a menace to democracy, but there is a silver lining in the dark cloud of his reign. This election has made clear the fractures in the democratic system; it has brought to light the fact that many of what we take for norms in government bureaucracy are principles that rely on an unwritten social contract. It is a system based on trust—we expect those we choose to lead us to honor the laws as written and also honor the spirit of governance.

For example, freedom of the press is part of the First Amendment of the Constitution. The people expect the White House to give daily press briefings and for the president to have regular press conferences, but Trump's White House has gone dark repeatedly. The people expect their leaders to not have conflicts of interest between their personal business and their public office, but Trump refused to hand over his tax returns, so no one knows whether economic policy decisions are being made with his own interests in mind as opposed to the people's.

In addition, unlike every president before him, Trump has not divested his business interests, which means that taxpayer money funds every visit he makes to a Trump-owned property, and it also means that those seeking to influence him can do so by spending money at his hotels. The people of the United States expect that their votes are counted properly, yet the president not only repeatedly called the voting system "rigged" during his campaign, but then went on to allege that there were millions of illegal votes and create a taxpayer-funded Commission on Election Integrity to prove his baseless voter-fraud conspiracy theory.

Trump's election has proven that the United States needs to take a hard look at the very foundations that are cracking under

Trump and then move to solidify them. No president whose finances are shrouded in mystery should ascend to the office. Voting is at the heart of the democratic process, and every citizen should be able to vote easily and freely. Even before the current talks of foreign interference in elections began, draconian voter-ID laws and gerrymandering had already disenfranchised millions of people, particularly people of color. There is no reason why citizens of a superpower like the United States should find it difficult to vote.

The times are dangerous, but I believe that the people of this great country will turn it around. Trump will become powerless in the face of a united populace defending its rights and its hard-earned democracy. Democracy is a shared experiment, but the truth is that it begins with personal responsibility. All of us have the responsibility to learn about the governing principles of the country, know our rights, and register to vote. Vote! Vote in every single election that you can—from the local to the national. Once you understand how the government works, you will see that every single election matters. Each citizen should know the names of and contact information for his or her elected representatives at all levels of government—call them and show up at their offices; they would like to hear from you.

In a democracy, knowledge and involvement mean power. Make a list of respectable objective news sources and support media with paid subscriptions if you can afford it. Read books on any subject. Books are good for the mind and the soul. Join groups of like-minded people in which the current political atmosphere can be discussed and how political issues are affecting the community. Volunteer wherever you can to help those less fortunate in society—a homeless shelter, an after-school program for children, a visiting program for the elderly, a center for the preservation of arts and culture. Lastly, be willing to show up for the issues that you personally care about, but also be willing to show up for others. When I say show up, I mean put your body in the street. In Mexico, protests are a way of life. When our people don't like something, the government hears it loud and clear because streets are shut down. Protests should always be peaceful. Life is precious, and violence only begets violence.

If you can't protest, use social media to let your voice be heard and to connect with others. Prior to Trump's election, there were people who had never made a call to their district or Senate representative, people who had never read the Constitution. Donald Trump has turned many of those sleepers into wide-awake social justice warriors. Democracy calls on us to believe in ourselves, to believe in each other, to always strive for peace, and to stay vigilant about this precious thing we call freedom.

CHAPTER 9

Spirituality
and the Way Forward

*"Today, more than ever before, life must be characterized
by a sense of Universal responsibility, not only nation to
nation and human to human, but also human to other
forms of life."*

—THE DALAI LAMA

I N 1974, I WAS named president of Coca-Cola's Mexico division
at the age of thirty-two, the youngest executive to reach the
top level. I was also married without children and considered
a hotshot at the world's most recognizable global brand. Those
were heady days filled with first-class travel all over the world to
meet with top financiers from Tokyo to Frankfurt, from London
to the famed Madison Avenue. We lived in Mexico City and
owned a boat, a motorcycle, a car, and a camper. Who could ask
for more? I was happy, of course, but I didn't feel fulfilled. There

was something missing, though I just couldn't quite figure out exactly what it was.

By the time my ten-year college reunion came around, I was ready to show off everything this farm boy had accomplished. I'd attended the Ibero-American University, a Jesuit college known to educate the children of well-to-do Mexican society members. The school's founding principle was based on St. Ignatius Loyola's teachings on being "men for others." I was certainly not a rich kid, although my family was better off than most and I had saved money from working on the farm under my father's regime. I lived on three pesos a day while in college and had to take three buses every day to school; often I would just skip the bus and walk an hour and a half so I didn't have to spend money. My class was presided over by Father Schiefler, a no-nonsense Jesuit priest whom I respected immensely, although I wish I'd gone to classes on time and been less distracted during lessons. The ten-year reunion would forever change my life.

The alums had rented out the flashy University Club in Mexico City, and we were all anxious to show off everything we'd accomplished since we last saw each other. Just ten years after graduating, many of the alums had already ascended to the highest positions of power in government and at Fortune 500 companies. We all arrived with our pretty wives, dressed in the finest clothes and dripping in jewels. We all laughed and caught up while drinking the best brandy there was, smoking cigars, and one-upping one another on our successes. It was the good life made even better by comparing it with others. Suddenly, Father Schiefler said, "I am totally disappointed in all of you...I wasted four years of my life on you." Our happy faces fell, the laughter stopped, and the room filled with an uncomfortable silence as tears ran down Father Schiefler's cheeks. He went on to say that he was sad that despite everything he'd taught us, we'd gone on to worship at the feet of business and enrich ourselves while the poor suffered in the streets. I was stunned. Father Schiefler sensed the hollowness I felt but couldn't really acknowledge.

The truth was at this point in my life, I thought what I really wanted, more than anything, was to be successful. Somewhere in the never-ending quest for material wealth and recognition, I had lost something or perhaps discovered there was something else I wanted more than being rich. I had not become, as Father Schiefler had taught us, a "man for others." Still, I went back to work and enjoyed a few more years of booming profits at a time in Mexico when the dictatorship's oil revenues were soaring and the economy was growing at 8 percent. Every now and then I would think about the Jesuit preacher's message. What was I doing? Was this what I was meant to do? By 1978, when I was thirty-eight, Coca-Cola presented me with an opportunity to move to Miami as president of the entire Latin American empire. This was it. The big one. The American Dream. My boss and mentor, Ted Circuit, assured me that by the time I was in my forties, I would be president of Europe or Asia, or even North America. My family, who'd ingrained in us the idea of doing our absolute best regardless of the task at hand, whether milking cows or selling soda, would be so proud of me.

I thought about my wife and myself going to Miami, starting anew, all of the things we would see and experience. Yet, none of it felt right. Faced with the opportunity of a lifetime, I searched my soul and finally realized that what I really wanted was to go back home. My boss was incredulous—he thought I was crazy to walk away from the keys to the Coca-Cola kingdom to grow broccoli and milk cows on my family's farm. I tried to explain to him that I needed to figure out how to be a man for others, and he replied that I was already being a man for others by working at Coca-Cola. Coca-Cola hired thousands of employees and gave truck drivers like I once was opportunities for growth.

On many levels, he was right. There was plenty I could do as a high-level executive, but corporate philanthropy wouldn't fill the void in me, because I'd finally figured out what the void was. It was the friends I'd grown up playing with who were now toiling on other people's farms trying to raise families of their own and barely making ends meet. I missed my other friends who'd crossed the southern border rather than stay and live a life locked into poverty and never-ending struggle. It didn't matter how smart they were, how compassionate and funny. They would never have the same opportunities I did, simply because they had been born into abject poverty.

At this point, I wasn't sure exactly what my purpose was, but it wasn't supposed to be that of a jet-setting executive. My mentor was disappointed, but I could no longer ignore the pull back to the land of my birth. What I needed was to literally and symbolically be brought back down to earth. And so I followed the Roman Catholic roots instilled in me since birth and the founding principles of the Jesuit order of St. Ignatius Loyola— we cannot ever be truly happy unless we seek happiness for others—and I went home.

Besides Brazil, Mexico has the largest population of Catholics in the world. Despite how deeply embedded Catholicism is in society, Mexico's political history and traditions prohibit the president from expressing religious faith in public. I believe in the separation of church and state, but I also believe that leaders should be guided by the moral principles of their faith. If we don't act from high moral principles, what else is there to guide us but earthly material gains? When someone is in a position of power, purely secular goals of control, fame, money, and resources lead only to corruption. In my memoir, *Revolution of Hope*, I wrote that "no cause is closer to God's will than the spiritual imperative that we love all people, treat others as we would like to be treated, and give every human being equal rights and equal dignity."

I believe it even more fervently today. I am a devout Catholic, and I take pride in my Catholic upbringing. The church has had a profound impact on my life and has given me a set of values I hold dear. This is not to say that I believe religion, in general, is the key to saving the world, but what I do believe is that there are fundamental universal themes found in all religions that could pave the way toward a new way of thinking about ourselves and grappling with the problems of the world.

In order to fight for human rights, you must believe in a shared humanity, regardless of individual religious beliefs. The belief that we are equal, that all humans deserve love and the right to live in peace, comes from faith. Loving others, tolerating differences, having decency and integrity are the universal values held in all religions. These are the universal principles that will bring people of all faiths, atheists and agnostics, together.

There is an anthropological theory that religions originated from stories humans told each other. The ultimate purpose of these stories was to create a shared goal that would keep order within tribes. As the tribes got bigger, the stories got more and more elaborate, a mixture of real-life events and mythology that were eventually codified into religious texts. Regardless of what one personally believes in, we know the moral principles found in religions have buttressed social justice movements that have helped end slavery and bring about civil rights. We also know that religion has been used to sow discord and justify the slaughter of innocents and unbelievers.

Politics and religion are similar in that both are frameworks that show us how to live—they can be tools of massive social change or instruments of perpetuating the status quo. Religions and political ideologies give us hope and also ask us to accept what already is. Both can, at times, keep people in a kind of caged perspective beyond which they cannot explore or see the logically fallacy in the narrative. Wars have been and are still being fought over different interpretations of the same religion. As the world and thus cultures and religions come closer together because of globalization and climate change, the more we become interconnected, unyielding religious ideologies cannot promote or keep the peace. The other reality is that in the struggle to hold on to the principles of freedom enshrined in liberal democracies, such as inalienable human rights, freedom of expression, and economic prosperity for all, we keep coming up against the rise of populist nationalist movements based on fear of change that are incompatible with democracy.

President Bush and I both came from the right side of the political ideological spectrum. We were both pro-life and believed in fiscal responsibility. Yet, I was to the left of Bush because I also believed in social safety nets like welfare and universal healthcare. Bush was an evangelical and a deeply spiritual and compassionate man; I was a devout Catholic—we were both Christians, but there were some fundamental differences in our interpretations. As both a Mexican and a Catholic, I find the death penalty abhorrent. Bush was staunchly pro–capital punishment. Mexico does not execute its citizens, and we have funds in place to help the legal defense of those facing a death sentence in the United States. I even refused an invitation to George W. Bush's ranch in 2002 to protest the execution of a Mexican national in the United States. I never understood how President Bush could oppose abortion on the basis that all life is sacred but argue in defense of the death penalty or support a military invasion that would kill thousands of innocents.

Beyond President Bush, I found it perplexing that God-loving Christians would rabidly scream for a border policy they knew would cause migrants to die of thirst in the desert or be abused by coyotes (smugglers) who extort and sometimes kill them. These same people would passionately argue about the sanctity of life yet vote to deny medical care to another human being based on legal status. I believe my Christian faith requires me to seek peace, to value and protect life, to be compassionate and to help my neighbors regardless of who they are or where they come from. I know these same universal principles are found in Islam, Judaism, Hinduism, Buddhism, and most all other religions of the world. I know this because I have been afforded the opportunity to meet people from all walks of life and because of my access to a quality education. In other words, my tolerance and understanding stem from knowledge and exposure to others and having an open mind.

Mother Teresa was a Christian who sparked a revolution of compassion by caring for the poor and the "untouchables" in society. Pastor Jim Jones was a Christian preacher who won the Martin Luther King Jr. Humanitarian Award and was responsible for the Jamestown massacre. Osama bin Laden was a Muslim man educated in the West who eventually became the mastermind behind the 9/11 terrorist attacks. Muhammad Ali was a Muslim man and world-renowned athlete and peace advocate who was sentenced to jail for five years (though he did not serve time as his case was appealed) in the prime of his career for refusing to fight in the Vietnam War. The idea of even placing the names of Mother Teresa and Pastor Jim Jones or Osama bin Laden and Muhammad Ali together seems ludicrous—as does calling all practitioners of a religion "evil." There are those who actively lead their lives based on the universal principles of faith, and there are those, like Jim Jones and Osama bin Laden, who pervert religion and use political ideology to divide rather than unify—those are the false prophets.

All false prophets create a heightened sense of looming danger that allows them to consolidate power to a tragic end. Historically, the reaction of the panicked people is to retreat to their respective "tribes," and there you see the rise of protectionism, nationalism, populism, xenophobia, nativism, racism, misogyny, and homophobia, with the corresponding reactions of increased hate speech and violence toward anything perceived as "foreign." It is a self-perpetuating, self-fulfilling cycle. Right now, the false prophets of the world are fueling a narrative about the clash of civilizations—Judeo-Christian civilization versus Islamic civilization. Today, Trump is the West's most powerful false prophet.

Trump advances the narrative about the clash of civilizations in various ways—first, it's his imagined "war on Christmas." During campaign rallies Trump would tell supporters that they were forced by "political correctness" to say "Happy holidays," and would promise them that under his administration they would be able to say "Merry Christmas" freely. The truth is there is no war on Christmas, and people are free to say whatever they want. His rhetoric was a thinly veiled dog whistle to Christian extremists signaling that their religion was under attack.

Trump's talks of bringing back "religious freedom" do not advocate freedom; he is aiming at asserting Christian dominance. But that is profoundly antidemocratic, because the Constitution gives all U.S. citizens the right to worship whatever god they want or to not worship at all. When Trump says he doesn't like hearing "Happy holidays," what he is deriding is the idea of tolerance that comes along with saying "Happy holidays," so that everyone, regardless of faith, is included in the statement. He is belittling a universal term that has arisen in social discourse that allows humans to speak to each other across religious divides. This attempt at a breakdown of civility is dangerous in a pluralistic society and in a world that is increasingly interconnected and where the challenges are global in scale—climate change, nuclear proliferation, poverty, disease, and violent religious extremism affect every corner of the world and require that humanity strive to find ways across divides.

Donald Trump paints himself as the strongman Christian savior, who has come to rescue and protect the flock from evil, but the more appropriate image for him is that of a wolf in sheep's clothing. Somehow, Trump appears to have the full support of the Christian Evangelicals, whose core principles of "family values" seem at odds with Trump's actual words and deeds. It was surprising to see a rise in Christian fundamentalism in the United States, to see this push to engrave religious views into secularist territory. To us in Mexico, the United States always seemed to lead the world in the culture wars, with the legalization of gay marriage and with increased protection of women's rights and racial and ethnic minorities. Trump's election signified a violent U-turn away from the politics of tolerance and inclusion that made the United States the leader in human rights advocacy around the world.

This abrupt U-turn happened in former communist Russia and is now threatening emerging democracies around the world. This U-turn is called the nostalgia effect, and it is a familiar story in Latin America, where the people would elect a progressive leader who ran on a platform of free-market social democracy that would emulate the United States and then, not long after the leader was elected, the people would become afraid of what lay around the corner, and the uncertainty made them long for traditional state-controlled mindless protectionist policies.

I've lived for three-quarters of a century, and though I cherish my Catholic faith, I have seen and read enough about the world's history to say these days I believe less and less in dogmas and more in the universal principles that will guide us toward peace. The basic truth about peace is that it begins within ourselves—we each must do what we can to instill in ourselves and our children, in our families, friends and peers, the core values of tolerance, decency, respect for others, compassion, and empathy. Our values have to shift away from the mindlessness of consumer mentality and toward our shared humanity.

I have seven basic spiritual principles I try to live by:

1. Love—the essential human impulse to want what is best for others. Everything we hope to accomplish, everything we build, must be done from a place of love. There is a nearly universal description of love in all major religions as the state of being patient, kind, without anger, without pride, without selfishness. Love does no harm. Love is hope.

2. Truth—we must seek knowledge and speak and live with one another in truth. We cannot continue to place ideology above facts and reason.

3. Integrity—the state of decency, fairness, and sincerity.

4. Compassion—we need to always use the power of imagination to place ourselves in another person's shoes. There is no love without the ability to be compassionate, to see outside of our own situations. To be able to understand another's pain as if it were our own. We would be slower to anger, to greed, to jealousy, if we looked at one another with love and compassion.

5. Responsibility—I do not believe I was born in this world to lie, to cheat, to steal from others. I believe that I came to this earth with an obligation to myself, to my family,

my community, my country, and to the world. If we do not have a sense of responsibility for our own actions as well as a feeling of obligation toward others, then we will fail as a human species.

6. Purpose—I think the word "purpose" is a magical word, a powerful word. There is no form of life or material on this earth that does not have a purpose. Everything has a purpose—from the most mundane activities to the most complicated. One must always question one's own actions and figure out what the goal is.

7. Performance—for me, this is the way in which you achieve your purpose. It's great to have a goal, but you must find the way to get there. What do you need to do to accomplish what you set out to do? In other words, performance is your life's checklist. The checklist will change, but it is the framework for your life.

Love, truth, integrity, compassion, responsibility, purpose, and performance are the way to peace. I believe that peace is the most sublime of all the universal values. Humans must search for peace and harmony, constantly, every second of every day. Without peace, we are in a state of conflict, in a state of war— both within and outside ourselves. Human beings cannot live in a state of peace if they are living in fear of violence or bombs, if they are worried about their health or their shelter. Imagine having to make breakfast or go to work while there are people shooting each other outside of your house. Those who live in war zones, those who are sick and hungry or homeless can never be at peace. This is how people are living all around the world right now. Without peace, there is no real life. True happiness will come when we live in love and peace. What greater thing could there be?

When we sign up to a specific political party and religious ideology, we are forced to exchange freedom of thought for a very specific set of principles. For example, in the U.S., I imagine it would difficult to be a Republican and also believe in gun control, climate change, taxing the rich, and solving society's ills through big government safety programs. Similarly, it would be challenging to be a liberal and be pro-life and believe in deregulating guns and fiscal responsibility. Same with religions; once you are born into a particular faith, you either follow the code as it is taught and interpreted by its earthly representatives or become a heretic. But the world is moving away from dogmas. There is so much knowledge available that our brains find it difficult to be confined by narrow definitions of life or fear of heaven and hell any longer. Every day we discover new things in the world of science and technology that move us forward, but we must be prepared to meet the challenges ahead with clear, level-headed thinking and relentless education based on the universal principles of love for our neighbor, compassion, integrity, truth, tolerance, and compassion toward humans and animals.

When it comes to faith, thousands of years' worth of wisdom can be found if we just concentrate on the overlapping principles found in all religions. Every day, we watch people murder each other in the name of God, led by false prophets who use religion as a sword to control, divide, and subjugate people based on their gender, race, class, and sexual orientation. As the world gets closer together through globalization, as we make room for those who are fleeing war and starvation because of climate change and geopolitical strife, we are called upon to look beyond the earthly imperatives of material gain and the false sense of security that lies in racist, xenophobic, and religious intolerance, and embrace the spiritual imperatives of religious principles—love for others, respect, tolerance, and peace.

What we need is a revolution of morals, of ethics, of love. I dream that world leaders can perhaps one day convene a sort of "Spiritual United Nations" that will guide our diplomats based on a moral compass rather than their narrow political interests. This idea runs counter to those who believe faith-based thinking has no place in politics, but we need to create a space where leaders are encouraged to think beyond the relentless pursuit of wealth, power, and greed. Leaders need to stop negotiating only in terms of winners and losers and dividing the world according to clashes of civilizations—accomplishing peace should always be the heart of every deal.

CONCLUSION

The American Dream: Out of Many, We Are One

D ONALD TRUMP IS A prolific liar, but of all the lies he has told, the most painful, divisive, heartbreaking of all was during his presidential candidacy announcement speech. Trump claimed that the American Dream was dead. Those words coming from a potential leader of the wealthiest, freest country on earth reverberated around the world, causing shock, horror, and sadness. The Founding Fathers must have rolled over in their graves. To say the American Dream is dead is to betray those pioneering men and women fleeing persecution who first touched upon America's shores with only the hope of freedom in their hearts. Trump has betrayed every man and woman throughout history who risked their lives thereafter to travel to this country and rolled up their sleeves and built it.

How many men and women have died in service to the United States? How many stationed all over the world have dedicated their lives to protecting this dream? Trump's lie betrayed the single greatest document of governance created—he betrayed the words in the Constitution of the United States: "We hold these truths to be self-evident, that all men are created equal, that they are endowed by their Creator with certain unalienable Rights, that among these are Life, Liberty and the pursuit of Happiness." To say the dream is dead is to betray every single man and woman alive in the United States today—the people who keep the country moving forward in thousands of different ways, from the food delivery person to the doctor, from the coal miner to the teacher, the farmer to the engineer, the mothers and fathers trying to steer their children on the right path. To this day, I cannot believe that Trump saying "The American Dream is dead" was not the end of his circus show.

Those who, like Trump, cloak their bigotry and nativism with phony anti-immigrant statistics don't realize it's the Statue of Liberty, not a racist wall on the southern border, that symbolizes the hopes of America. The America that became the most powerful country on earth by opening its arms to the poor, the huddled masses yearning to breathe free, will not crown the Statue of Liberty with barbed wire or replace her torch with a guard tower's searchlight. To those who think a wall will protect the American Dream, I have news for you: dreams do not flourish inside walled compounds. Walls will not keep America safe; they will only keep America locked in. If history teaches us anything, it teaches us that people will not live forever behind walls, because walls are an affront to our shared humanity. Walls are not created to protect us; they are created to keep us apart.

The world has moved on from the fossilized thinking of Trump and his cohorts; there are no walls high enough to keep out the rush of new ideas, and not enough border patrols or customs agents to keep out those who are willing to work their fingers to the bone for a better life. Trump doesn't really want a wall; he wants a cage. A prison whose borders will suffocate the American Dream, holding it hostage to fear, hate, greed, and indifference to the plight of its neighbors. You see, the American Dream was never about the riches of a big house or a white picket fence. The American Dream has always been about democracy. America cannot abandon us now just when so many around the world have seen the light of freedom and are willing to fight to bring democracy to their country.

The American Dream is what makes America great. Immigrants from all over the world came together to birth the revolutionary idea that out of many, we are one. The pioneers all shared an inner force, a power within them to reject oppression and create a better life for themselves and for their families. Those who cry that the country belongs to them, unless they are Native Americans, would be wise to remember they are the descendants of immigrants. America does not belong to any one people, and the only ones who can claim a longer tenure on the land are Native Americans, who deserve dignity and respect.

Today's immigrants and refugees are no different than those original pioneers—whether from Ireland or Nigeria, Syria or India, Jamaica or Mexico, Colombia or China, Sudan or the Dominican Republic, all are willing to leave their home to get to a place where they sometimes cannot speak, read, or write the language, because they believe in the promise of America. Immigrants work hard for their families, and their work helps the country prosper. To hear immigrants speak of the United

States is to see the beauty of patriotism. The American Dream is theirs too.

As president, I traveled the world to promote Mexico's democracy and Mexico's interests—from the White House to the Kremlin, from the Vatican to Castro's dining room, from Tony Blair's fireside to Nelson Mandela's offices. I have gone from Presidential Palaces to slums, spoken with Chinese farmers, Arab leftists, African dignitaries, those who are rich and those who are extremely poor. I have had the privilege of access to so much diversity in the human condition. I know that Trump and his supporters are wrong—they are wrong that the world is laughing at America; they are wrong that the American Dream is dead. The world loves America. People everywhere dream about America, marvel at the ideals of the Founding Fathers, admire the Statue of Liberty, and look on in awe at the ideas of religious liberty and freedom of speech and the notion that every single human being is created equal.

The American Dream of democracy is alive. Those who are currently speaking out against the forces of tyranny in Venezuela know it is alive because they see it on their television screens and read it on their smartphones. Youths and opposition leaders are being jailed, shot at point-blank range, and run over with military trucks at this very moment because they want to preserve democracy. The dream is real, and we must do everything we can to keep the light of freedom alive. The key is for us to come together as nations to fight poverty and ignorance instead of fighting wars. We should build schools and hospitals instead of walls. We cannot remain indifferent to the widening chasm between the rich and the poor and the looming threat of climate change. We have access to the best minds in science and engineering to help fix these problems, but we must not let political and religious ideologies divide us. Franklin D. Roosevelt said, "Every gun that is made, every warship launched, every rocket fired signifies, in the final sense, a theft from those who hunger and are not fed, those who are cold and are not clothed. This world in arms is not spending money alone. It is spending the sweat of its laborers, the genius of its scientists, the hopes of its children."

The United States is, in a way, not so much a country as it is an ideal. Regardless of everything that has happened in American history, despite the legacies of genocide, slavery, racism, homophobia, and misogyny, this country has been able to legislatively course-correct in only two centuries, whereas other societies have spent thousands of years fighting about these things. America's ability to make those sweeping social justice changes so quickly is what makes the country exceptional. The American Dream is really humanity's dream. It is a global dream. Every single person, whether born in the United States or elsewhere, every single one of them searching, reaching ever higher for the opportunity to better themselves and their families, is deserving of respect and admiration. That constant striving for the better is what makes America's heart beat.

The American Dream is one of the best hopes of humankind on this earth. And no one, certainly not the so-called president of the United States, can remove that dream from the hearts of billions of people around the world. The need for freedom and hope, the desire to have a safe home, cures for illness, a good education, a good job, time to create art—these are basic human needs that cannot and will not ever be stopped by bans or by walls. What we need are bridges—bridges of understanding, of partnerships, friendships, and knowledge.

I haven't given up on my dream that one day the United States will return to the spirit of compassion and cooperation found in the Marshall Plan. As populist demagogues rise in Latin America, the United States should learn from the lessons in the past and see that the only way to both maintain the spread of democracy and ensure the continued prosperity needed for peace is to widen NAFTA so that it includes all of the Americas. This is the way to compete fairly with the economic giants in the Asian continent. The United States needs to look to the south and see that a union with the entire American continent will lead to the world's largest economy. I disagree that good fences make good neighbors. The truth is that the universal spiritual values of helping your neighbor and treating others as you would like to be treated are the only way to make peace.

As continents are brought together through globalization, the American Dream requires us all, in every corner on earth, to work together. We are facing the existential challenge of climate change that may bring with it more famine, more war, more forced displacement, and other unimaginable horrors. We must all rise up to meet the challenges ahead together, with love and fellowship toward one another. This requires cooperation, understanding, and tolerance. I am committed to using the power of my voice to help the United States get rid of Trump and his administration, and I am committed to getting rid of false prophets like him all around the world. But removing false prophets is a short-term solution to the problems of inequality that lead to their rise.

I believe the core of humanity is good. Only the inequalities exacerbated by unyielding political and religious ideologies can make us turn to our worst human impulses. The feelings of envy and greed take over when a person measures poverty based on another's wealth, or ignorance based on another's education, and sees the world only as a zero-sum game. Each of us is born with unlimited potential, but we are the products of our parents, our communities, and our governments. We need to address the widening divide between the rich and the poor, and enact policies that acknowledge our shared humanity. We need to turn away from false prophets and seek leaders who embody universal values in word and deed. The true leaders, leaders who have galvanized humanity, leaders who have made us reflect and have opened our hearts—those are the ones who embody all the universal ideals of tolerance and respect for human rights. Mahatma Gandhi toppled the British Empire with the strength of his words. Lech Walesa brought down the repressive regime of the Soviet Union in Poland. Nelson Mandela transformed South Africa's history of apartheid. Martin Luther King Jr. changed the way people thought about race. Hillary Clinton, despite all who vilified her, has lived a life of service to the public and became the first woman to win the presidential nomination by a major political party. Clinton didn't win the presidency but, because of her, there is a girl out there who now believes she can.

We must focus our eye on the present and the future, so we prevent the rise of more Donald Trumps in the world. False prophets like Nicolas Maduro of Venezuela, Recip Tayyip

Erdogan of Turkey, Rodrigo Duterte of the Philippines, el-Sisi of Egypt—all will one day meet Lady Justice in their own country or join other exiled ex-dictators dodging extradition warrants. The United States has allies all over the world waiting with bated breath for the ship to right its course and America to return to the promise it holds. The United States may not be seen as the Leader of the Free World while Trump is at the helm, but Angela Merkel of Germany, who said we must be "united in the trust that it is not isolation and the building of walls that make us successful, but an open society," France's Emmanuel Macron, and Canada's Justin Trudeau are showing the world that compassion toward immigrants and refugees is the only way forward.

Do not fear Donald Trump. Fight. Don't give up. Never give up hope. Never give up on the American Dream. History is on our side. Have faith in each other. There is something good happening out there. I can feel it. Trust me, I helped usher in democracy in Mexico, so I know what momentum feels like. For millennia, those in power have used politics, skin color, sexuality, and religious faith to repress and divide, but it's getting harder to convince people of these lies. It is impossible to both believe in the American Dream of democracy, the idea that all are created equal, and also swallow the myths of division.

When I visited America as a teenager, I was hurt by the racism of some, but I was more inspired by the generosity of many. I went back to Mexico with something in my heart that no one could take away, something that stayed with me and flourished and, along with my spiritual beliefs, finally pushed me to leave the comforts of a corporate job and dedicate myself to public service. That thing was the idea that all of us are created equal, that all of us deserve opportunity and happiness and respect, and that we cannot remain indifferent to the evils of religious persecution, poverty, slavery, and tyranny that drove people out of the old world and are threatening to destroy this new one.

We will move on from the false prophets, but it's going to take all of us raising our voices, confronting ugly lies and painful truths. Hillary Clinton was right—we are stronger together. Donald Trump thinks he can wear us out with his constant falsehoods, and rob us of the capacity for outrage at his utter incompetence and repeated cruelty toward women, immigrants, and refugees, those who are LGBTQ, the poor, the elderly, and the disabled. But Trump would do well to remember that he did not win the popular vote. There is a powerful majority of the country actively resisting his politics of disunity. Those who haven't woken up yet, will. The Resistance is getting bigger, and every single day new people join the battle cry. Already they have defeated Trump's attempt to rip healthcare away from millions of people, and through the sheer force of public pressure, a grand jury has been impaneled to investigate Trump and his cohorts of financial crimes. There is a revolution of hope happening in hearts everywhere. More people are moving away from the ancient hatreds of envy, greed, and ignorance taught out of fear.

Unlike my predecessors, those dictators of old who took their riches and lived in exile, I continue to live in my home state of Guanajuato, Mexico. I am signing off from my grandfather's Rancho San Cristobal, where Marta and I have finally opened Centro Fox, an academic center that houses my presidential library and a think tank along with the headquarters of our

Vamos Mexico foundation. We decided not to go quietly into our sunset years, and instead continue to help build the new world. We plan to work as long as we can promoting global democracy and social justice. We invite artists and thinkers from all over the world to come and show us, and those less fortunate, how to make the world a better place for all. We hope our efforts prove that good people coming together can do more than all the empty rhetoric of false prophets who prey on the ignorant and the poor. I will never stop believing in our shared humanity. You are welcome to come visit us anytime. As we say in Mexico, "*Nuestra casa es su casa*"—our home is your home.

Yours in Resistance,

Vicente Fox
President of Mexico (2000–2006)